D0387764

BUILDING A MAGNETIC CULTURE

BUILDING A MAGNETIC CULTURE

How to Attract and Retain Top Talent to Create an Engaged, Productive Workforce

KEVIN SHERIDAN

New York Chicago San Francisco
Lisbon London Madrid Mexico City Milan
New Delhi San Juan Seoul Singapore
Sydney Toronto

The McGraw-Hill Companies

5 6 7 8 9 10 QVS/QVS 19 18 17 16 15

ISBN: 978-0-07-177399-7
MHID: 0-07-177399-1

e-ISBN: 0-07-177511-3
e-MHID: 0-07-177511-0

This publication is designed to provide accurate and authoritative information in regard to the subject matter covered. It is sold with the understanding that neither the author nor the publisher is engaged in rendering legal, accounting, or other professional service. If legal advice or other expert assistance is required, the services of a competent professional person should be sought.

—From a Declaration of Principles Jointly Adopted by a Committee of the American Bar Association and a Committee of Publishers and Associations

Library of Congress Cataloging-in-Publication Data

Sheridan, Kevin, 1960-
Building a magnetic culture : how to attract and retain top talent to create an engaged, productive workforce / by Kevin Sheridan.
p. cm.
ISBN-13: 978-0-07-177399-7 (alk. paper)
ISBN-10: 0-07-177399-1 (alk. paper)
1. Personnel management. 2. Employees--Recruiting. 3. Employee selection. 4. Employee motivation. 5. Organizational behavior. I. Title.
HF5549.S552 2012
658.3--dc23

2011044681

McGraw-Hill books are available at special quantity discounts to use as premiums and sales promotions, or for use in corporate training programs. To contact a representative, please e-mail us at bulksales@mcgraw-hill.com.

This book is printed on acid-free paper.

I first give special thanks and recognition to Ms. Amelia Forczak, one of HR Solutions' Rock-Star and Highly Engaged employees; without her creativity and undying research efforts, Building a Magnetic Culture *would never have been published. To my parents, and especially my dad, who taught and inspired me to be passionate about what I do for a living, and instilled in me both an iron-clad work ethic and the perseverance of never giving up easily. A deep thanks to my wife and children for their love and support throughout the peaks and valleys of the last year. Finally, I have never-ending gratitude to the many employees and clients of HR Solutions, who chose to create, contribute to, and remain with, our Magnetic Culture.*

CONTENTS

INTRODUCTION

To become the best in the business, it is essential to employ the best people. A phenomenal team of dedicated employees is truly the foundation for supreme organizational success. While most managers wouldn't argue with this viewpoint, one particular question is harder to agree upon: *How* do employers build a staff that is ready and able to take the organization to the next level?

The answers lie within this book.

Through 20+ years of Talent Management consulting, conducting hundreds of thousands of employee focus groups with a vast array of organizations, and analyzing the results of millions of employee surveys, I can honestly say the best employers have *a lot* in common. Whether they have 25 employees or 250,000, the basic elements for successfully attracting, retaining, and engaging employees are much more similar across the board than one might think. While specific Talent Management strategies vary throughout different organizations, top employers reach a higher level of success because of their ability to build a *Magnetic Culture®*.

A Magnetic Culture *draws* talented employees to the workplace, *empowers* them, and *sustains* an environment in which they are *more likely* to stay. Such a culture is marked by *engaged employees* who share a strong desire to be part of the value the organization creates.

Although employees are endlessly unique in their personal preferences and goals, there is an overwhelming commonality in the aspects of the workplace that are most closely tied to Employee Engagement, and thus, contribute to building a Magnetic Culture. These similarities hold true for employees across a range of demographics, including age, sex, ethnicity, education level, and tenure at their organization. Commonalities also exist in organizations of all sizes, in a wide range of industries, located all over the world. Considering the multitude of employers and employees, it would be easy to assume one Talent Management strategy wouldn't fit all. While this may be the case, a Magnetic Culture *does* fit all.

In the following pages, this book illuminates exactly why some organizations become Best-in-Class® and others struggle to stay afloat. Success doesn't happen by chance; it is achieved through basic cause-and-effect relationships. There are certain workplace practices that are powerful cultural magnetizers and others that act as detrimental demagnetizers. The first step to making positive changes at your organization is simply to gain a better understanding of how these elements come into play. Every action made by employers impacts their employees' perceptions of the value the organization provides. To attract, retain, and engage top talent, you have to offer more value for employees than other organizations. The myriad of ways in which an employer can offer value are the building blocks of creating a culture that is truly magnetic.

Actionable best practices that have been proven to increase Employee Engagement and lead to better business outcomes are found throughout this book. Case studies of top companies and exclusive interviews with seasoned industry leaders allow readers to learn from the best of the best. Additionally, readers will become privy to a revolutionary new concept that is changing the traditional, and, I believe, antiquated approach to Employee Engagement. This concept, in itself, has been the difference maker for many organizations in creating an environment where employees *actively contribute* to cultural magnetism. Since a major challenge lies in not only creating a Magnetic Culture but maintaining it as well, this new concept makes it much easier for employers to *sustain* a magnetic environment. The ideas in this book provide you with the insight you need to get ahead and achieve greater business outcomes for your organization. In the chapters ahead, I will help you gain a deeper understanding of exactly how you can attract, retain, and engage top talent and form a solid plan to make your organization the best in its business. Creating an environment where engaged employees thrive is the basis for success overall and will help you build your own unique Magnetic Culture.

Chapter 1

WHAT IS A MAGNETIC CULTURE AND WHAT ARE THE BOTTOM LINE BENEFITS OF EMPLOYEE ENGAGEMENT?

You can take my business, burn up my building, but give me my people and I'll build the business right back again.

—HENRY FORD

Engaged employees possess an intellectual commitment and emotional bond (e.g., pride, passion, enthusiasm) to their employer, an eagerness to exert both extra discretionary effort and creativity, as well as a willingness to accept some personal ownership for their own level of Engagement, all leading to maximized outcomes for customers, the organization, and themselves. Engaged employees are likely to recommend their organization as an employer of choice, as well as promote the organization's products and/or services. Employee Engagement matters. Engaged employees are[1]:

- *Ten times* more likely to feel good work is recognized.
- *Ten times* more likely to feel Senior Management is concerned about employees.

- *Eight times* more likely to feel their supervisor encourages their growth.
- *Seven times* more likely to feel they receive regular performance feedback.
- *Four times* more likely to be satisfied with their job.
- *Four times* less likely to think about leaving the organization.

Engaged employees are also linked to satisfied customers at a Pearson correlation coefficient of $r = +0.85$, meaning that these two variables are strongly related.[2] A *Pearson correlation coefficient* is a mathematical index used to describe the direction and size of a relationship between two items or variables. A correlation can range between –1.0 and 1.0, with –1.0 being a *perfectly negative correlation* (every time one item increases, the other item decreases, and vice versa) and 1.0 being a *perfectly positive correlation* (both items increase and decrease together). A coefficient of 0 represents a completely random relationship. Most items measured using this scale fall somewhere in the middle of –1.0 and 1.0, but rarely exactly on 0. It is important to note that this correlation does not imply causation. Instead, it shows the relationship between two variables. In essence, the more engaged employees you have on your team, the more satisfied customers you will have as well. When it comes to Employee Engagement, there are three types of employees in the workplace: actively engaged, ambivalent, and actively disengaged. Understanding these levels of Engagement and how they affect one another is essential to managing an engaged and productive workforce.

Actively Engaged Employees

- Go above and beyond, frequently doing more than what is asked of them

- Are net promoters: they proudly represent and promote the company's brand
- Are passionate about the mission, vision, and values of their organization
- Have awareness and personal commitment to their Engagement level
- Are self-motivated and driven to perform at a high level
- Are welcoming and supportive of new employees
- Contribute new ideas, often, to better the organization
- Adapt to and facilitate change
- Are optimistic about their future with the organization

Ambivalent Employees

- Are not apt to "go the extra mile"; they do what is asked of them and are not inclined to do much more
- Volunteer rarely, if ever, for extra assignments or to take lead roles
- Display lower energy and lackluster performance on assignments
- Focus, day to day, on simply "getting by"
- Can often feel unappreciated or unimportant
- Go to work primarily for the paycheck
- Are more likely to have a haphazard attendance record and "watch the clock" for the time their shift ends
- Are not overly excited about their current work situation

Actively Disengaged Employees

- Have negative attitudes about their employer and job duties
- Are malcontent; they sometimes openly show their distaste while on the job
- Focus on problems

- Can cause more harm than good with their behavior and actions
- Are not personally invested in the success of the organization
- Badmouth supervisors consistently behind their managers' backs, either in the workplace or to friends and family
- Actively seek to share their negative personal viewpoints with new and ambivalent employees

Figure I.1 summarizes the frequency of Engagement levels in the workplace.

Figure I.1 Employee Engagement Levels in the Workplace

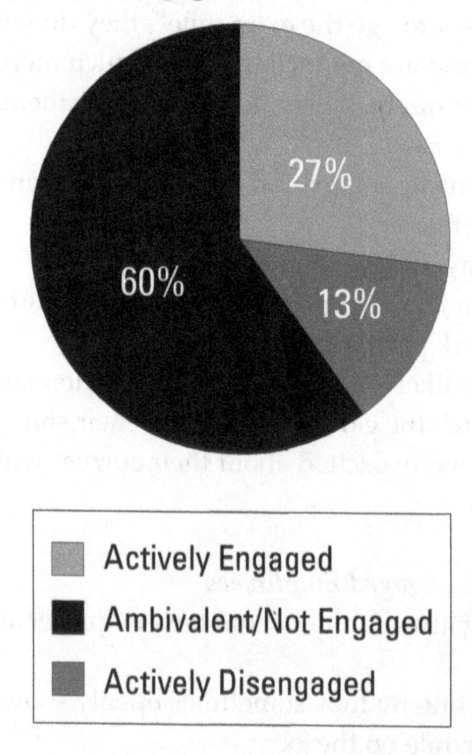

Source: HR Solutions' Normative Database, https://actionpro.hrsolutionsinc.com (normative items; accessed May 25, 2011).

The Spread of Engagement Levels

People are often influenced by those around them, and the workplace is no exception. While many think the social pressure to adopt other's viewpoints ends after our teenage years, that certainly is not the case. My grandma actually used to say one of the great benefits of getting old is *"There is a lot less peer pressure."* That always made me laugh heartily, but she definitely made an important point that transfers to the workplace. Although managers cannot completely control the spread of Engagement levels at their organization, they can make decisions that will promote an increase in Employee Engagement.

Ambivalent employees are the most easily influenced by their coworkers' Engagement levels, so pairing them with engaged employees for group projects and assignments is a great tactic to increase Engagement. Engaged employees generally enjoy being leaders and mentors, and will set a great example for Ambivalent employees to take personal ownership of their Engagement level.

Actively disengaged employees can be toxic to other employees, especially those who are ambivalent. Other organizations, such as Gallup, have deemed disengaged employees to be workplace "vampires" who suck the life out of those around them. When ambivalent employees befriend disengaged employees who are infectiously negative about their position and the company, that negativity will spread like cancer. Since misery loves company, disengaged employees often seek out other employees and drag them into the malaise of negativity. Managers should also be aware that these vampire-like employees can quickly suck positivity from coworkers if given the chance.

Casey Stengel, baseball Hall of Famer and former manager of the New York Yankees and New York Mets, has a quote that hits this situation right on its head: *"The secret of successful managing is to keep the five guys who hate you away from the four guys who haven't made up their minds."* It sounds like a funny strategy, but it honestly works when it comes to Engagement. Managers should try to limit the interaction between disengaged employees and ambivalent employees, as well as new employees. Instead, encourage all employees to get to know the employees who are engaged. Engaged employees aren't negatively affected by their colleagues' Engagement, so it is a good idea to use them as mentors.

Actively disengaged employees are prime candidates to consider transitioning out of the organization. Millions of managers waste boatloads of time coaching these Engagement arsonists, hoping for improvement to no avail. Venturing down the path toward yet another coaching or disciplinary review session, managers are falsely optimistic that meaningful improvement will occur. In reality, this is taking managers away from spending valuable time with their A Players. It is often better to cut your losses and spend more time with the employees who are deserving of the coaching, mentoring, and development, than deal with the entirely disengaged.

In order to protect the workplace environment from negativity, sometimes it can be best to simply get rid of the source of the problem. Do not count on disengaged employees to show themselves to the door; research has shown they are likely to stay, although they produce the worst outcomes for your organization.[3]

Actively managing the Engagement bookends is a critical step toward building a Magnetic Culture. Identifying how employees with different levels of Engagement affect one another is crucial for heading down the path to organizational success. Creating a workplace environment where Engagement thrives and Disengagement dies should always be a management priority.

Figure 1.2 Linkage between Performance Evaluations and Engagement

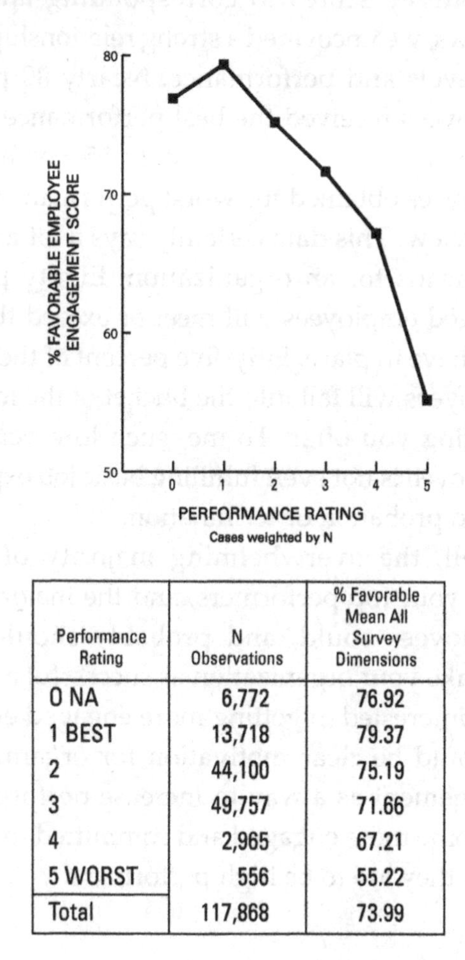

Performance Rating	N Observations	% Favorable Mean All Survey Dimensions
0 NA	6,772	76.92
1 BEST	13,718	79.37
2	44,100	75.19
3	49,757	71.66
4	2,965	67.21
5 WORST	556	55.22
Total	117,868	73.99

Performance

Although it is widely believed that engaged employees produce a higher quality of work than ambivalent and disengaged employees, I wanted to see data to understand exactly how Engagement impacts the bottom line to statistically prove whether Engagement initiatives will have a return on investment (ROI). Personally, I am a numbers guy.

By correlating 117,868 of our clients' individual Employee Engagement Survey scores to corresponding annual performance reviews, we uncovered a strong relationship between Engagement levels and performance. Nearly 80 percent of engaged employees received the best performance rating on their annual evaluation. Approximately 55 percent of disengaged employees obtained the worst performance rating on their annual review. This data certainly says a lot about what Engagement means for an organization. Eighty percent of the time, engaged employees will meet or exceed the highest standards you have in place. Fifty-five percent of the time, disengaged employees will fall into the bucket of the lowest performance ranking you offer. To me, such low performance means an employee is not even fulfilling basic job expectations and is subject to probation or termination.

In a nutshell, the overwhelming majority of engaged employees are your top performers, and the majority of disengaged employees could, and probably should, be terminated. To make your organization as successful as possible, you should be interested in getting more engaged employees. This study should be clear motivation for organizations to focus on Engagement as a way to increase performance. As employees become more engaged and committed to their jobs, the more likely they are to be high performers.

Engagement and Repeat Customers

On average, it costs five times more to attract a new customer than to retain a repeat customer.[4] Customers come back when they are satisfied with their experience and the level of service or product quality they have received. Employees' interaction with customers, therefore, plays a crucial role in whether customers will want to return. In fact, customer service can be more important to people than the actual product or the convenience of doing business with the organization.

For example, suppose you live near two dry cleaners that provide the exact same quality in cleaning and tailoring. One dry cleaner is right around the corner from your house, but the employees are not at all friendly. They make you feel like a burden when you come in, and they take their time before helping you because they are not concerned with making you wait. The other dry cleaner is a mile away, but the employees are extremely nice, remember your name, and seem genuinely happy to see you. They also provide speedy service because they care about respecting your time. Which business are you going to frequent?

Think about how the situation would change if both dry cleaners had equally friendly employees, but one business had a higher quality of cleaning and tailoring because employees cared more about doing a good job. I bet you would probably go to the dry cleaner that provided a better quality service, even if the dry cleaner was slightly less conveniently located.

Customers are faced with decisions like this hundreds of times each day. Research has shown that 70 percent of buying experiences are based on how customers feel they are being treated.[5] In addition, about 90 percent of unhappy customers will not buy again from the company that disappointed them.[6] In a world with so many options for any given product or service, Engaged employees will set your business apart and give you an edge on the competition.

The Power Dimensions and Becoming Best-in-Class

Our organization considers clients Best-in-Class when they score in the top 10 percent favorable for overall scores from their Employee Survey. Earning such favorable scores is no easy feat; we have millions of responses from thousands of organizations in our Normative Database, so the competition is stiff. Gaining Best-in-Class status means that employees responded in the top 10 percent favorable of all organizations. Best-in-Class organizations have the most Engaged staff overall, but we wanted to see what else they have in common.

We analyzed Best-in-Class survey data by *dimension*, which is the general topic that survey items are grouped under. Our survey dimensions are as follows:

Dimension 1: Overall Job Satisfaction
Dimension 2: Satisfaction with the Work
Dimension 3: Coworker Performance/Cooperation
Dimension 4: Pay Satisfaction
Dimension 5: Benefits Satisfaction
Dimension 6: Promotions/Career Advancement
Dimension 7: Supervisory Consideration
Dimension 8: Supervisory Promotion of Teamwork and Participation
Dimension 9: Supervisory Instructions/Guidance
Dimension 10: Communication
Dimension 11: Human Resources/Personnel Policies
Dimension 12: Concern for Employees
Dimension 13: Productivity/Efficiency
Dimension 14: Training and Development
Dimension 15: Physical Working Conditions
Dimension 16: (Concern for) Customer Service
Dimension 17: Strategy and Mission
Dimension 18: Job Stress
Dimension 19: Importance to Job Satisfaction and Employee Productivity

Out of all of these dimensions, we found a glaring similarity between Best-in-Class organizations that was completely absent from non–Best-in-Class organizations. Every single one of our Best-in-Class clients scored above average on the same three dimensions:

Dimension 10: Communication
Dimension 16: (Concern for) Customer Service
Dimension 17: Strategy and Mission

Not one of the hundreds of HR Solutions' clients was subpar or at a deficit to the norm on these three key components of a Magnetic Culture. It is not a fluke that so many world-class and crème de la crème organizations have the exact same things in common. It shows that these three ingredients are a crucial part of the recipe for a highly productive, engaged Magnetic Culture. We call Dimensions 10, 16, and 17 the *Power Dimensions*.

Another distinctive quality our research uncovered about Best-in-Class organizations is that they can charge *10 percent more* than other companies (without adversely impacting revenue growth) and commonly make twice as much in profit. While price and quality are important purchasing factors, these profits come from employing a great staff that has the organization's best interest at heart.

Disengagement = Bad PR

The importance of Employee Engagement has been amplified by social media. When customers or employees are unhappy with an organization, it is now easier than ever before to spread that message to hundreds, if not thousands of people within mere seconds. This general principle is called "the Multiplier Effect." On average, one happy customer will tell five other people about his or her experience. Thus about five others will learn of the compliment. On the flip side, one unhappy customer will voice his or her dissatisfaction to 10 potential customers who, in turn, will tell at least five other people. Thus about 60 others will eventually learn of the complaint. Essentially, bad news travels faster and farther than good news.

When social media is involved, however, the message spreads exponentially. Think about how easy it is to post a status update on Facebook that says you went to a new restaurant in town. Whatever you think about the new business becomes an instant restaurant review for all of your friends. If you had a great time, your friends might consider going there. If you experienced bad food and rude employees, your friends will likely avoid the restaurant if they remember your comments. More than ever, people are starting to rely on customer reviews as major influencers in consumer purchases due to the widespread capabilities of social media. As an organization, this means it is essential that employees provide excellent service to current customers to build the pipeline for future customers.

United Breaks Guitars

Perhaps you are familiar with the *United Breaks Guitars* YouTube video. This video, which has had over 10 million hits, chronicles the real-life experience of how David Carroll had his guitar broken by careless employees during a trip on United Airlines in 2008 and the subsequent reaction from the airline. The song immediately went viral when it was released in 2009, and it was a public relations humiliation for United.

Carroll alleged that he and fellow passengers on board the flight witnessed the baggage-handling crew throwing guitars on the tarmac. Sure enough, when Carroll arrived at his destination, he discovered his $3,500 guitar had indeed suffered a broken neck. In his song, he sang that he "alerted three employees who showed complete indifference." Carroll filed a claim with the airline but was denied compensation because he failed to make the claim within 24 hours of the incident. This is when Carroll decided to use the Multiplier Effect to rectify the problem. Through his video, he succeeded in "paying United back" for how their employees previously treated him and his belongings. The video got so much attention that United's overall reputation was severely damaged—all due to a few disengaged employees' actions.

If the employees who had been handling Carroll's baggage were engaged in their jobs, they would have been much more careful. They also would have been aligned to United's mission and corporate responsibility, which states, *"As a company, we realize that the actions we take and decisions we make matter."* The baggage employees would have thought about how the way in which a guitar is handled matters to the customer and the company, and they would have been more careful. The employees who were notified of the situation would have realized their response to Carroll mattered as well, and they would have done more to rectify the situation and provide better customer service. This is a perfect example of how the minor actions of employees can forever alter an organization's path.

United finally apologized to Carroll and said they would like to use his video to train employees on how *not* to handle customers' baggage. Hopefully they are focusing on Engagement in their training initiatives as well.

The Perils of Disengagement: A Personal Case Study

Sometimes we end up learning from our own mistakes. This can often be the most painful way to learn something but certainly a way in which the lesson is driven home, never to be forgotten. I learned an extremely painful lesson on Engagement recently, and I would like to share it as a mini-case study, in hopes that it will help others avoid the same detrimental repercussions of employee Disengagement.

When it comes to Talent Management, I like to give people the benefit of the doubt. I believe most people are good human beings by nature, and that you can trust others to behave ethically and legally. I also genuinely believe people can improve themselves with coaching and mentoring, as this is oftentimes the case. However, I have learned there are certain situations in which the smartest thing you can do as a manager is to watch for red flags and listen when your gut tells you something isn't right.

The Accountant

Our organization had employed the same accountant for seven years. When I hired her, I knew she came from a troubled family with members reportedly in prison or suffering from drug addiction, and she was trying to rebuild a healthy and productive life for herself. I fervently believe in the American Dream and providing opportunity to others. There is no doubt that my experience as a young white minority growing up on a Native American reservation heightened my sensitivity about restricted access and opportunity; it instilled in me both an innate appreciation for diversity, as well as a strong desire to both help correct inequities and provide opportunity to others. Hence I wanted to help give this accountant that opportunity, and I was rooting for her to succeed. In essence, I let my personal feelings cloud my judgment and perception of her less than stellar work performance.

As an employee, at the start she was average. She definitely had areas in which she could make improvements, but I overlooked some early red flags and performance problems.

As time transpired, her work became worse and worse. Disturbingly, she began to cover up her mistakes and performance problems by misrepresenting events and playing the "blame game." Employees noticed her behavior and began to question why someone like that should be part of our team. On more than one occasion, an employee or manager suggested she be terminated.

Ultimately, an employee caught the accountant fabricating an e-mail to cover herself for something she had forgotten to do. I confronted her directly about lying and asked why I shouldn't fire her. She burst into tears, profusely apologized, and explained how she "never" lied like that. She begged me to understand that it was an isolated mistake that would not happen again. Since the actual lie involved something relatively minor, I decided to give her a second chance. If I could go back in time, I would have fired her right then and there. A lie is a lie. People who tell one lie are bound to tell more.

Our accountant managed payroll for our entire staff, as well as accounts receivable and accounts payable. She provided me with hard copies of all of our bank and company credit card statements, payroll deposits, and summaries from our accounting software program, which I spent a great deal of time each month scrutinizing and checking for accuracy. I used to be an auditor, and after assiduously and consistently reviewing the large stack of printouts she gave me on a regular basis, it appeared as though she had our company finances under control and there was nothing out of the ordinary that I needed to worry about. I trusted she was doing the job, partly due to the repeated best-practice advice I had given to countless executives—about the importance of trusting your employees, giving them the freedom to succeed in their job and do what they do best—in short, proven architectural DNA for building a strong Magnetic Culture.

The Acquisition

At the end of 2010, we were targeted for acquisition by a global Human Capital Management consulting and tax/audit organization that could benefit from our normative database and proprietary action-planning software, and we could benefit from gaining a larger global presence. It truly seemed like a great match for both parties, and I was as excited as ever about the opportunity. I was especially keyed up for two main reasons.

First, we would be taking our game "global," something HR Solutions could not do on its own.

Second, we had secured really great jobs for 30 of our 37 employees, a pretty remarkable feat in any acquisition scenario.

We began working hard to finalize the deal by the end of the year to avoid a large capital gains tax increase that would come into play on January 1, 2011. Our accountant started playing a key role in the merger, especially in the financial due diligence process of the acquisition, at which point her performance really started to drop. She said she thought she would be terminated from her position if the acquisition went through, but that would not have been the case. Ensuring that our staff members' jobs would be secure through the transition and in years to come was a top priority. An accountant would have been an easy fit with the company planning to acquire us, certainly much easier than some of our other positions held by employees that I was intent on keeping.

However, instead of proving herself to be a valuable employee who the other company would want to keep on board, she started dragging her feet on the completion of work assignments and the acquisition due diligence. She called in sick several times, took unauthorized vacation days, and missed important deadlines—all hallmarks of a disengaged employee. She claimed to be having health problems that were being aggravated by the extra work and stress of the upcoming partnership. I put her on probation and considered firing her, but felt we needed her to complete the financially related due diligence requests. In addition, I had the feeling that the "problem" would go away naturally after the acquisition. I wanted to be sensitive to her personal issues, but it began to seem as though she was simply doing everything in her power to delay the acquisition. On more than one occasion, she exclaimed, "What am I getting out of this [the acquisition]? What is my motivation?"

We managed to complete the due diligence process right before the end of the year, and the deal was finalized. We planned to announce the great news to our whole team on January 4, 2011.

On January 3, 2011, the organization with which we were merging received an anonymous letter that brought the deal to a screeching halt. The letter made wildly false accusations that attested to our lack of organizational integrity and ethics, in a wide variety of completely fabricated claims. The acquiring organization's executive team brought the letter to my attention immediately. I was absolutely floored. Sixteen years of building a great brand and company on the eve of bringing its sale to fruition all came to a grinding halt due to a fraudulent anonymous letter.

While the claims in the letter were totally false, the writer had enough knowledge of our business and the merger that it seemed like it could only have been written by one of our own employees. I asked myself how it would even be possible for one of my staff members to do something so malicious, especially after I had laboriously worked the staff's job security into the agreement; in essence, I put people before money. What made the situation even more troubling and confusing was that very few of our employees even knew the merger was happening. This knowledge was only granted to Senior

Leadership and the accountant, which consisted of four people in addition to me. I trusted all of my Leadership Team, so I was at a total loss on who could have written the letter.

I explained that all of the claims were untrue and, quite frankly, ridiculous, and offered complete indemnification to the acquiring company for any and all of the baseless claims and threats in the letter. Yet, without an explanation or an admission of guilt from the writer, our potential partner decided to back out of the deal in light of the bizarre situation. After recovering from my initial shock and overwhelming disappointment, I decided to dig deeper to understand why this atrocity had happened and find out who was responsible.

The Investigation

I hired a private detective to investigate the situation. The typed letter arrived by mail from a Northwest Chicago suburb, and the return address was a fake post office box. Since there was no handwriting or electronic trail, the letter was essentially untraceable. We conducted a search through our computer servers and found no trace of the letter being written on company computers. We did not have much to go on, but kept investigating any and all potential leads.

While all of this was taking place, I started to notice suspicious behavior on the part of our accountant. She had already been put on probation for performance issues, and the probation was extended at the beginning of December when she took a sudden and unauthorized one-week vacation to Jamaica. It was akin to a quarterback leaving the field to take an early shower with two minutes left in the fourth quarter of a tied, season-ending championship game. Thus began more suspicions that the accountant was not only failing to support the game at hand, but in fact was not even playing on the same team.

Most pointedly, after six months of her daily inclusion in the due diligence for the deal, she returned from the New Year's holiday and never once asked what happened to the merger when we did not announce it to our staff on January 4, 2011. The other three Senior Leaders all asked why the staff meeting had been cancelled, as it was obviously a very pertinent topic. Even after all of the daily due diligence requests to her from the M&A lawyers, investment bankers, and the acquiring company went stone-cold and ceased to exist, she said nothing and asked nothing. In addition, her general work performance went from questionable to abysmal. She wasn't processing forms accurately or on time, and our staff had started to complain about not being able to rely on her for important items. She also frequently began to "act out" her aggression in inappropriate ways that disturbed her coworkers.

After careful deliberation, I decided termination was the only reasonable option. I stood in her office for two hours while she gathered her things and eventually left, mumbling something about filing a complaint with the Equal Employment Opportunity Commission (EEOC). It was only when she finally left that office that I started unlocking and going through all of the file cabinets.

The Findings

Right away, I discovered something was very wrong. One file drawer was completely stuffed full of unopened mail. I looked at the postmark dates and they seemed to go back to the beginning of time. Apparently she had been hiding the mail whenever she didn't feel like opening it and had been doing so for years. Upon digging through the drawer, I found checks from clients that had never been cashed, IRS tax refunds that were never deposited, late notices for bills that had not been paid, thank-you letters from interviewees that I had not hired because they didn't send a thank-you note, and a wide array of other important items. I was hoping this would be the low point of my discoveries, but it only got worse.

One of my initial discoveries cast me back four and a half years when the accountant came into my office in a flood of tears exclaiming that her father had just dropped dead of a heart attack. Naturally, I consoled her at the time, offered her more time off, and asked what else I could do to help her in her time of need and mourning. She looked at me and said, *"I can't give him a proper funeral and burial. I don't have the money."* I said to her, *"That is the last thing that should be on your mind right now. How much do you need?"*

I agreed to loan her the $10,000 she said was needed to cover the costs of the funeral services and burial. One of the things I have prided myself on the most as a leader and executive is to really be there for my employees in their time of personal need or suffering. I wrote the check. I attended the funeral.

Now, four and half years later, I stood in her former office looking at a copy of a check for $7,900 to HR Solutions, a supposed partial repayment check for the loan I gave her. I asked myself, "Why would she make a copy of this check? She either made the repayment or not." Although I had personally seen the accounting entries in our system for the repayment amounts, I now became concerned that she had falsified the repayment entries and that in fact, she had never deposited any of the checks into the HR Solutions' bank account. Sure enough, our bankers verified that no such deposits were ever made.

I then began to audit *everything*. I had already personally checked each payroll every two weeks for the past 16 years, so I was sure there wouldn't be any problems there. Much to my chagrin, I was wrong again. Our accountant had been secretly running phantom payrolls to herself on the side; she simply omitted those hard copies from the stack she gave me to review. On one of the payrolls, she had collected a $10,000 bonus in this fashion, and had gotten away with it.

Next, I started checking through our credit card statements. At this point, I was downright scared of what I might find. Although I had carefully reviewed each monthly statement for each credit card since our founding in 1995, I was looking at the hard copies she gave me. Once again, I found she had been using the company credit card for personal purchases. Amazingly, she had actually used her company credit card to fund part of her unauthorized vacation to Jamaica.

How did this escape my careful reviews? She actually removed the pages covering her fraudulent card charges, restapling the entire American Express bill before giving me the statements for my review. I thought I was reviewing the statements in their entirety, so it never occurred to me to log on to our online account to double-check.

The Costs

In retrospect, I should have more carefully ensured the accuracy of information I was receiving and reviewed all financial information directly online, rather than through online printouts given to me. This troubling situation is currently being investigated by the Chicago Police Department, and of course, people are considered innocent until proven guilty in a court of law; however, our former employee is facing counts of trade libel, torturous interference, and breach of fiduciary duty.

I wanted to share this story with you to prove a point about the perils of Disengagement, both the financial and emotional costs. Do not underestimate the liability of employing people who do not clearly and visibly have your organization's best interests at heart. Disengaged employees can truly damage your business, almost to a point beyond repair. Thankfully, our accountant clearly did not cause everything we have built up to crumble to the ground, but she certainly altered the course of where we were headed. Actively disengaged employees, such as this one, literally demagnetize a Magnetic Culture.

It is just like Jim Collins said in his revolutionary book, *Good to Great: Why Some Companies Make the Leap . . . and Others Don't*, you have to "get the right people in the right seat on the bus" so you can drive it where you want to go. If you have the wrong people on the bus, they will take you in the wrong direction.[7]

Since our accountant has left the organization I am confident we are back on the right path. We have the best group of employees I ever had the pleasure of working with in the years since I started our company. Success is all about people; if you employ amazing people, everything else will fall into place. If, for whatever reason, you tolerate underperformers and people you are fundamentally uneasy about trusting, you and your organization will suffer the costs.

Everyone Benefits from Employee Engagement

When employees are fully engaged, individual employees feel fulfilled and satisfied in their careers, organizations increase productivity and quality, and customers enjoy a better product or service, possibly at a better price.

A perfect example of how we all benefit from Engagement can be found in the health care industry by examining the linkage between engaged employees and hand washing compliance.[8] It is a scary truth that approximately 1.7 million hospital-acquired infections occur each year, leading to approximately 99,000 deaths in the United States alone.[9] Research shows that an individual is five times more likely to die from seeking medical care than to be killed in a homicide.

An extremely common way to cause infection is through unclean hands. Depending on the facility, employees are asked to adhere to a certain sanitation policy. The word *asked* is important in this context because employees can choose whether or not they wish to follow the organizational procedure. Hand washing requires extra work on behalf of the employee. Depending on his or her personal feelings regarding how much effort to put forth in the workplace, hand washing efforts could be outstanding or abysmal. Employees face hundreds of choices every day. They are constantly given the opportunity to do their best, but it is up to their discretion on whether or not they will. When it comes to hand washing, we thought employees' level of Engagement would be an excellent indicator on whether they will put forth the extra effort to wash their hands as often as asked by their employer.

We decided to ask employees confidentially about their hand washing compliance, and correlate that data to their level of Engagement from an Employee Survey. We found a near-perfect correlation coefficient ($r = + 0.99$) between hand washing compliance at health care facilities and Employee Engagement. The positive Pearson correlation does not conclusively show that Engagement causes hand washing compliance. However, one can easily see how employees who are committed to doing a great job and are aligned with the organization's mission of healing patients would make more of an effort to follow procedures that are proven to make a difference. In this industry, Engagement doesn't just lead to loyal customers, it saves lives.

Engagement affects your bottom line in every way imaginable, and it is essential for building a Magnetic Culture. If you want to improve any aspect of your organization, I would be willing to bet that it is somehow connected to Employee Engagement.

Chapter 2

ENGAGEMENT IS A TWO-WAY STREET: EIGHT STEPS FOR CREATING AN ENVIRONMENT OF SHARED ENGAGEMENT

Problems cannot be solved at the same level of awareness that created them.

—Albert Einstein

Is it five o'clock yet? As a manager, that is probably not your favorite thing to hear around the workplace. Although employees show up on time and get their work done, many are counting down the hours, minutes, and seconds until they can go home.

Wouldn't it be great if employees enjoyed their job more? As a manager, there is only so much you can do to motivate an employee who has no interest in being an engaged employee. The real solution is that the employee must want to be more engaged. When the responsibility for increasing Engagement is shared, outcomes are much more favorable for both the employee and the employer. Thus, it is critical for staff members to understand the personal benefits of being engaged employees.

All too often, the focus of Employee Engagement centers on how it will improve the organization. While it is true the organization will benefit greatly from a more dedicated and committed staff, employees will want to know what is in it for them. Why should they work harder just to make the company more successful if they will not see any direct benefit from such improvement? The truth is employees *will* benefit directly from being more engaged; they simply need to understand *how*.

Educating employees on what they can gain from improving their Engagement level is often the missing piece of the Talent Management puzzle. There is considerable irony in how employees have historically been left out of Employee Engagement initiatives. As one of our clients aptly pointed out, leaving employees out of Employee Engagement is the ultimate oxymoron. Organizations need to create a means for staff members to understand their Engagement level and how they can make improvements. Managers should make employees comfortable discussing challenges associated with Engagement. In a perfect world, all people would go to work with a great attitude every day, regardless of what was going on around them. In reality, this cannot be expected. Every job inevitably has its high and low points. It does not matter how much people love their organization or position, there will be times when their Engagement is tested. It is how people handle the low points that will ultimately determine their mettle and ultimate success.

Handling the Low Points

When I was much younger, my friend got me a job working for his dad. It was blue-collar work, and we specialized in a variety of trades, such as plumbing and electricity. Since these were practical skills to have, I felt fortunate for the opportunity to learn, as well as make some money during college summer breaks. Overall, I enjoyed the job, but I will never forget the day my motivation and determination were put to the ultimate test.

Our company was called by a local kindergarten that was having serious sewage problems. For those of you who are not familiar with working around and with sewage systems, it can be much worse than you probably even imagine. I will try to spare you most of the details, but that week I could have starred on Discovery Channel's *World's Dirtiest Jobs*.

Shortly after on-site arrival and investigation, we determined the holding tank for waste had become backed up due to an electrical failure of the pump within the holding tank. The only way to fix the problem was to empty the tank, and in doing so, allow for someone to get inside the tank and check the pump for the source of the electrical failure. Much to my initial horror, my boss recommended me for the job. I certainly had no desire to complete such a foul task, but it was something that had to be done. The kindergarten could not operate without a functioning sewage system, so I felt the importance of getting the job done quickly and effectively. I also knew how rare it was for us to have an assignment that was this terrible, and I would gain some respect from my boss and colleagues if I was able to rise to the occasion. I made the decision to simply suck it up and do it.

I would like to say I valiantly completed the task, but in reality, I threw up three times before I could even get all the way in the tank. I was determined though, and I refused to give up before fixing the problem. I was told the tank had been cleaned out, but that was the furthest thing from the truth. I ended up being ankle deep in sewage, with more of it dripping onto my head from leakage above. The work boots and rubber gloves my company had given me for protection did virtually nothing to shield me. Also, the fact that it was 90 degrees that day, with absolutely no ventilation, certainly did not help the situation. The problem with the pump was so catastrophic we learned it would take a full week to fix.

I wore my own clothes at work, and rather than ruin all of them, I wore the same shirt and pair of jeans every day while working on the holding tank. When I went home, I peeled them off at the end of my driveway and left them there until the following morning. The worst part of those days was waking up and changing back into the excrement-hardened, crusty clothes. The first day, I brought my lunch, but soon realized I was too grossed out to eat. Rather than take any breaks, I worked straight through each shift, simply trying to finish the task as quickly as possible. It was, to this day, the most disgusting job I have ever done.

After I finished the job, the staff at the kindergarten was extremely grateful. They would once again be able to use the restrooms at the facility and the deplorable smell would soon subside. Although the execution of the job was not at all enjoyable, it felt good being able to help the staff. My co-workers and boss also gained a new level of respect for me; my boss especially did so, since he took the liberty of watching me much of the time from the comfort of the sidewalk 20 feet from the holding tank. I proved to them I was committed overall, and did not let the day-to-day frustrations keep me from working hard. The difficulty in successfully completing the task ended up making it more rewarding. It certainly was a once-in-a-lifetime experience, but best seen in my working life's rearview mirror.

I like to use this example in consulting because it can really put things into perspective for people. While some jobs have lower lows than being surrounded by sewage, I think it is safe to say that most do not. If you can continue your focus on the big picture during temporary low points, before you know it challenges will pass right by and the "average" workday will begin to look absolutely stellar. This is truly a better way to live life in general, not just in the workplace.

I firmly believe that a large part of one's Engagement stems from personal choice. I believe that each of us wakes up in the morning empowered with the choice of approaching the day and our job with either optimism and Engagement, toxic negativity and Disengagement, or the "time to make the doughnuts" attitude in the middle.

I have a very special appreciation for this as an entrepreneur. Anyone who has started a company from scratch could spend hours reciting all of the challenges and barriers he faced threatening the ultimate success of his venture. Almost every successful entrepreneur I have known will credit his success to determination and perseverance during the times when all indications were that the venture was doomed to fail. One of my favorite phrases in the Japanese language is *Ganbatte kudasai,* which means "Good luck" figuratively, but "Persevere" literally. Indeed, *"Luck is the point at which Opportunity meets Preparation,"* a quote attributed to many people, from Seneca, the first-century Roman philosopher, to Chicago's own Oprah. Think about it. Do you make an effort to make your own luck or are you waiting for it to appear from out of nowhere?

New situations pose new challenges. Acceptance of the new challenge begins with choosing an attitude of dealing with it. Instead of choosing the road to victimhood and self-depreciation, we can be comforted by the serenity prayer or something like it: "God, grant me the serenity to accept the things I cannot change, the courage to change the things I can, and the wisdom to know the difference."

We know our kids might do drugs. We know how tough the economy is and that we could lose our job. We know we could get terribly sick, even in light of the healthy habits we live by. Thus, instead of being a prisoner to these subterranean worries, it is far easier and liberating to let go by admitting we are not in control of any of these tragic possibilities.

"The wisdom to know the difference" at the end of the serenity prayer does not have to invoke negativity. The sailing quote by author William Arthur Ward sums it up quite well: "The pessimist complains about the wind, the optimist expects it to change, and the realist adjusts the sails." Have you adjusted yours to tack toward Magnetism and Engagement?

Building Healthy Relationships

The effort people put into relationships should be a two-way street. Whether it is family, friends, clubs, or community, people must *give and take* to maintain healthy relationships. If a person is always taking and never giving back, others will likely feel the relationship is unbalanced and unfair to them. Although these ideas on balance in relationships are a social norm, in the context of work relationships people often have a different viewpoint.

All too regularly, people have relied solely on their employer to keep them engaged in the workplace instead of taking any ownership of their own Engagement. With this mentality, employees think their employer is holding all of the cards, and if they do not like what they are dealt, there is nothing they can do to improve the situation. If employees become unhappy, they will often stay that way because they do not feel empowered to make any changes that would better the outcome, or they will eventually choose to leave the organization.

In the past, employers have primarily been responsible for their employees' Engagement. Unfortunately, this model rarely yields great results for the employee or the employer. Engagement is just like love; you cannot demand it from

Figure 2.1 The Lopsided Look at Employee Engagement

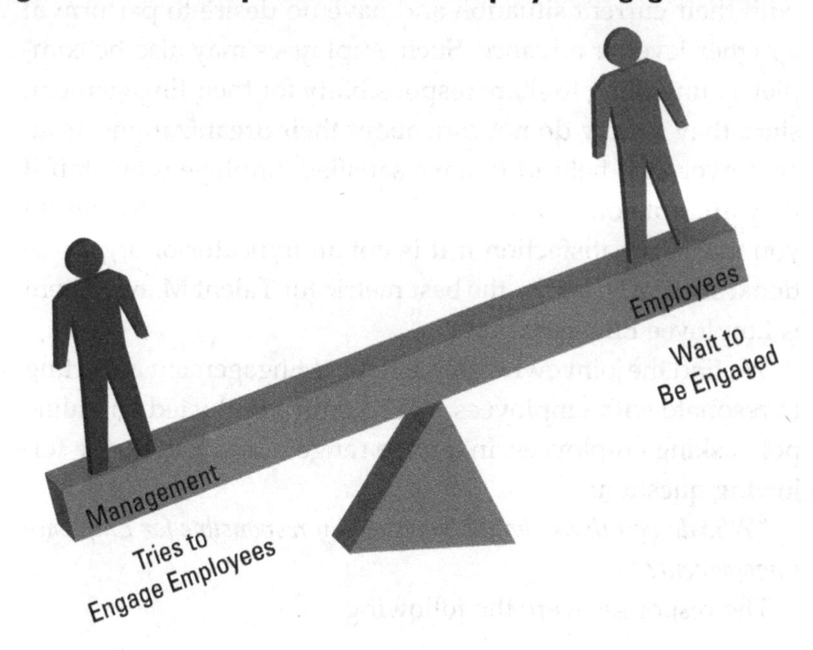

another person. Even while employers struggle to engage their entire staff, if employees feel they are not being engaged, they can become lethargic and withdrawn. It is time for the employer-employee relationship to mirror social norms that encourage equal give-and-take.

Employee satisfaction has been a popular Talent Management topic in past years, but Employee Engagement is actually a much more powerful indicator of employees' true relationship with, and contribution to, the organization. While satisfaction is a general indicator of mood or opinion, Engagement goes far deeper than that. Engagement ties to employee behavior and higher performance because employees care about the good of the company and doing their personal best. Satisfaction does not directly relate to specific behaviors or actions. Satisfied employees may be underperformers who are perfectly happy with their current situation and have no desire to perform at a higher level or advance. Such employees may also be completely unwilling to share responsibility for their Engagement, since they simply do not care about their organization. As an employer, is it helpful to have satisfied employees on staff if they are not contributing? Of course it's not. So why would you measure satisfaction if it is not an indicator of organizational success? Clearly, the best metric for Talent Management is Employee Engagement.[1]

We find the joint ownership model of Engagement is starting to resonate with employees. We recently conducted an online poll[2] asking employees, in a wide range of industries, the following question:

"Who do you think should be primarily responsible for Employee Engagement?"

The responses were the following:

- *Responsibility should be shared*—73 percent
- *Managers*—18 percent
- *Employees*—7 percent
- *I'm not sure*—2 percent

Despite the majority of employees believing the responsibility of Employee Engagement should be shared, most employees are either Ambivalent or Actively Disengaged in the workplace. There is clearly something causing a disconnect regarding employees taking action to increase Engagement.

For years, the path to Engagement has been a one-way road that only management could drive down. Why should management hold all of the responsibility for engaging their employees? The promising concept of joint ownership for Employee Engagement was completely missed by an entire industry (Gallup, Hewitt Associates, Watson Wyatt Worldwide/Towers Perrin [Towers Watson], Hay Group, Sirota, Valtera, *and* HR Solutions) for decades.

At the other end of the spectrum, some people believe 100 percent of the responsibility for Engagement belongs to employees. David Zinger, an Engagement expert, is of this school of thought. "There is no one but me who is responsible for my Engagement," he told me. While he agrees organizations and managers play a part in Engagement, in the end, employees are solely responsible for owning their Engagement. He believes leaders can help employees most by supporting them in making progress on owning their Engagement.

It is time for the path to Engagement to evolve and become a two-way street that employees and management can travel together. Empowering employees to take responsibility of their Engagement is the key to a Magnetic Culture.

Eight Critical Steps for Shared Ownership

Winston Churchill once said, *"We first shape our buildings; thereafter they shape us."* Nothing could be truer as it relates to shared ownership and accountability. Any organization hoping to build a Magnetic Culture should begin by constructing what I call "invisible organizational architecture." Within this framework, you can build a solid structure of ownership as a shared value.

For a perspective on why ownership is essential, consider the difference it makes in our actions. Have you ever gone out of your way to change the oil in a rental car? Of course not. You are a renter, not an owner, and as such, you behave like a renter. However, when you own a car, you *want* to make sure the oil is changed regularly so that it continues running in good shape for as long as possible. As an employer, you want your employees to think and act like owners. If you erect an Organizational Structure of Ownership, employees will exhibit the passion, pride, and loyalty that come with the character of ownership.

Managers and employees must address the imbalance of Engagement ownership in the workplace and take action for improvements. If employees do not get involved in the Engagement solution, they become part of the problem.

Step 1: Teach the Concept of Engagement

I truly believe the way in which people were raised has a monumental impact on their willingness to accept responsibility for Engagement. The values our parents instill in us as children play a significant role in how we view the world, what is expected of us by society, and what we should expect from ourselves. As a parent, I try to teach my two daughters the value of hard work and dedication. I have raised them with the notion they will be successful in life if they are committed to doing their personal best. My wife and I also give the girls chores to show them how important it is for everyone in our family to help out and work together as a team. These are the same core concepts people need to grasp to be happy and successful in the working world, so it is beneficial to introduce these values at a young age for them to stick.

I see how a person's background influences his or her work ethic every day at HR Solutions. Ashley, one of our employees, was raised on a family farm in Minnesota, where she grew up helping to plant and harvest the crops. Many families in her area had farms as well, and all of the kids started pitching in at a young age. It was commonly accepted that it was everyone's responsibility to help with the family business, especially at the culmination of the year when the crops had to be harvested.

A few years back, we encountered one of the busiest times in our company's history. We were completely inundated with requests for proposals, sales presentations, and client meetings, all within an extremely short time-frame. It was an exceedingly challenging time for everyone at our company, but I was confident it would lead to great things and bring in new business. I just needed to make sure my employees were willing to put in the extra hours to make it through the week. Most of the staff seemed to be feeling the pressure, but when I checked in with Ashley, she was calm, cool, and collected. *"Kevin,"* she told me. *"When it's harvest time, it's harvest time."*

This example of work ethic and taking personal responsibility for the success of the team was unbelievably admirable. Ever since that day, I realized I could trust Ashley to come through in challenging times, and she continues to be an integral part of our team. (My personal advice is that if you ever come across a Minnesotan farm girl in the recruiting process, you should consider her farming experience to be applicable to your business.)

Although some people will have a natural advantage in understanding joint responsibility due to their background, managers and employers are responsible for teaching all employees about Engagement. Many people are simply not familiar with the realm of, and signs of, Engagement. What may seem like a basic concept to more seasoned professionals is brand-new to some people. Employees will need to be taught what Engagement is, who is responsible for it, and why it matters. Managers should enlighten employees on what they have to gain from taking part in their Engagement.

Benefits of Taking Ownership for Personal Engagement

- Getting the recognition they deserve
- Helping develop a clear career path to promotions and advancement
- Making their job more interesting
- Learning how to work with a difficult manager and how to manage their manager
- Helping their managers understand them

- Procuring the resources they need to do their job and do their job well

When employees learn of the personal benefits of taking ownership for their Engagement, they are much more likely to actively participate. In addition, employees who share responsibility for Engagement will feel more in control over their future, which is highly empowering.

Case Study: "Ignite" Engagement

Dedicated to Advancing Wellness™ in both patients and employees, Hospira, a global provider of injectable drugs and infusion technologies headquartered in Lake Forest, Illinois, realizes the link between Employee Engagement and patient outcomes. In an exceptional example of considering the big picture, the organization has embraced the idea of joint ownership between managers and employees. With more than 14,000 employees globally, Hospira incorporates the untapped employee resource with a firm belief that Engagement should not simply fall to managers; rather Engagement involves a contribution from both management and their staff. As such, "Ignite" was born.

According to Ken Meyers, Senior Vice President and chief officer for Human Resources, Ignite is not simply a program, but rather a brand under which multiple initiatives for joint ownership of Engagement fall. In creating the brand, Pamela Puryear, Ph.D., Vice President for Organization Development, wanted to provide a way for employees to "connect the dots" across many employees facing programs which drive Engagement. Now, when team members see a program branded under the Ignite name, they are instantly aware of its relationship to them. Employees are encouraged to "spark the fire within" by owning their professional development and Engagement through Ignite.

Utilizing Ignite to inspire joint ownership is illustrated with two key programs:

- *Ignite Grant.* Approximately 40 grants, up to the amount of $5,000, are given annually to team members. These grants are awarded to employees who uncover an otherwise unmet learning and development need within the organization and detail a plan to resolve it. As Dr. Puryear sees it, employees are often the most qualified individuals to identify their own development needs, and the grant provides the funds to take ownership for meeting those needs. Joint ownership of Engagement is much easier to accomplish with the appropriate resources. When employees have the means to increase their contribution on the job, they will likely be more Actively Engaged.
- *Ignite Your Growth Toolkit.* This online career development and planning toolkit provides about a dozen easily accessible resources that employees can refer to at any time. The kit includes tools ranging from self-assessments to best practices for understanding each individual's unique Engagement level. The tools are available to Hospira employees across the globe and are used in collaboration between employees and their Leadership. Through the toolkit, resources are provided for employees to take ownership into their own hands.

With the overwhelming success of the Ignite brand thus far, Ken Meyers, Pamela Puryear, and other senior leadership at Hospira plan to continue igniting employees to embrace Engagement initiatives. The brand is indicative of an inspired method to invoke joint ownership of Engagement. With contributions from both ends of the spectrum, Hospira will likely continue rising in the realm of Employee Engagement.

Branding Engagement initiatives is a great way to boost awareness and understanding. Many employees will likely be surprised to learn that their manager and organization care about their feelings and opinions. For these employees, Engagement is not only a new concept, but a new way of looking at the working world.

Step 2: Help Employees Understand Their Own Engagement Level

It is possible to fully understand the concept of Engagement, yet fail to accurately interpret your own level of Engagement. Incorrect assessment is common and can happen for various reasons.

Since the thought of being disengaged can evoke a negative connotation, especially as it relates to work ethic, people can be naturally reluctant to qualify themselves in that bucket. In addition, people oftentimes do not recognize their own areas for improvement. For example, extremely negative people often do not realize they are being negative, but the people around them notice it quickly and easily. When managers describe characteristics and actions of different levels of Engagement, it can be easier for employees to gain a more accurate understanding of their own Engagement.

Another important factor in the confusion of personal Employee Engagement is that Engagement fluctuates. It can change greatly throughout the course of employment, and often does. Employees can have the tendency to *rest and vest*, a term often associated with the Silicon Valley boom in the 1990s. Employees who experienced that historical moment in time began to feel satisfied they were in a good place, which was certainly the case. As a result, many employees became complacent and stopped working to reach the next level. Soon enough, such widespread success ran out and countless "vesters" had a painful awakening when their organization was no longer growing, or in some cases, was no longer in existence. The organizations whose employees did not rest had a much better chance of maintaining success at the end of the era.

Employees frequently do not realize when their Engagement level has changed because they have already prequalified themselves into one of the three Engagement buckets—actively engaged, ambivalent, actively disengaged. Rather than acknowledging their personal change, they continue to believe they are on the same level. With this in mind, evaluating and truly understanding Engagement should be a continuous focus for employees of all levels and tenures.

Personal Employee Engagement Report

An excellent way for employees to find out their true Engagement level is through PEER®, the patent-pending Personal Employee Engagement Report, developed by HR Solutions in 2007. PEER revolutionizes the relationship between employees and managers by putting Engagement in the hands of employees. PEER is an optional and fully confidential report that not only highlights the employee's level of Engagement (actively engaged, ambivalent, or actively disengaged) but also makes useful subject-specific suggestions on how an employee can enhance his or her own Engagement in the workplace. Suggestions for specific action steps are based on how an employee responds to certain items in the survey.

For example, if an employee scores unfavorably in response to the item "My supervisor encourages my career growth," his or her PEER report would provide ideas for improving the career dimension of Career Development. Some suggestions are as follows:

- "Seek personal career guidance. Ask your supervisor about his or her own success stories and what has worked for his or her career growth."

- "If you have strong experience and an interest in developing others, ask your supervisor if you could be a mentor to new coworkers."

PEER helps employees receive personalized, actionable advice for increasing Engagement and is an excellent tool for supporting the process of joint ownership.

If you would like to receive a free trial of PEER to better understand your personal Engagement level, please visit **www.hrsolutionsinc.com/peer.cfm**.

Not all employees will embrace the concept of co-ownership for Employee Engagement. In fact, some will strongly eschew it. It may not be surprising that those most likely to reject responsibility for their Engagement are, you guessed it, the actively disengaged population.

Since PEER is typically optional for employees to take, of course there are individuals at almost every organization who choose not to participate. We can tell from the PEER Engagement demographics that those who do choose to take PEER are a much more engaged population than the general employee population. Forty-five percent of people who request PEER are actively engaged, compared to 12 percent who are actively disengaged.[3] For this reason, many organizations have started making PEER mandatory for their whole population, in an effort to truly educate and connect with their actively disengaged workers.

Step 3: Employees Should Brainstorm on What Could Increase and Decrease Their Engagement Level

Since people understand their own desires and motivation better than anyone else, employees are best able to determine the adjustments that would make a meaningful difference to them. Employees should think about all of the aspects of their position and workplace, and make a list of what they like best and what they would like to see changed. From major changes to seemingly insignificant adjustments, it helps to determine all influencers.

Employees should make suggestions on what they can do to increase their own Engagement. Maybe an employee does not like the job content of her current position, but she does not have enough experience or qualifications to be promoted to a different role. She can express her feelings to her manager and suggest a possible course of action to gain the necessary experience to move forward. Perhaps she can take a night course, or shadow a tenured employee who works in the position she aspires to fill one day. This work will be extra for the employee, but it could ultimately help her get a promotion where she will like the job content better, leading to higher Engagement.

If employees cannot think of anything at all that would increase their Engagement, sometimes it is better when they are "voluntold" to do something. In a nutshell, *voluntold* means volunteering a person for something without offering a choice in the matter. If you are a parent, chances are this is a skill you have already fully developed. When your kids complain about being bored, you might suggest they go outside and play. In some cases, you have probably insisted on it. This is for both their benefit and yours; you know they will find a way to entertain themselves when pushed to do so, and their change in attitude lifts a weight off your shoulders. It ends up being a win-win situation.

Oddly enough, the same concept can hold true for adults. Sometimes we need a little extra push to start working on what will ultimately increase our happiness. As a manager, you have the unique opportunity to put a stop to progress inertia by "voluntelling" your employees to start new initiatives that will likely increase their Engagement. In short, *re-engage* them. If employees are not satisfied with what they are voluntold to do, it is interesting to see how it suddenly sparks their imagination for other meaningful options. This is another win-win for you.

When employees come up with their own suggestions for increasing Engagement and follow through on their plans, it is a great example of how they can take responsibility to help facilitate change. Managers can't always wave a magic wand and give employees what they need to succeed (more education, training, experience, certification, etc.), but managers can support employees in their quest to achieve these goals. If an employee needs to leave a little early one day a week to make it to class, the manager should support Engagement by accommodating this need, as do most organizations with a Magnetic Culture.

Managers can help employees generate ideas by providing specific suggestions to get the ball rolling. Is there a certain task employees would like to do more often? Are there any supplies that should be ordered to help employees better do their job? Do they feel they could benefit from additional training? When employees identify specific ways to increase their personal Engagement, they are more likely to take ownership and create change.

Step 4: Employees and Managers Should Meet One-on-One to Talk about How They Can Support Each Other to Increase Engagement

Employees should not only determine what is affecting their Engagement, but also openly communicate it. Some changes will undoubtedly be imperative for removing the roadblocks to Engagement, and managers must understand their employees' feelings and opinions to take action. A great time to have these discussions is during performance reviews. For decades, organizations have conducted annual performance reviews of their employees to determine a variety of factors, such as compensation increases, promotions, and training/professional development needs. These conversations provide the perfect opportunity to discuss and examine Engagement, but most organizations are not capitalizing on them. HR Solutions' Research Institute estimates that less than 5 percent of performance reviews conducted by managers with employees have a component or discussion centered on the individual level of Engagement and the related gaps. Changes that would improve Engagement could oftentimes easily be made if they were simply brought to the attention of the manager. Mainly, Engagement should be included in performance reviews for the following three reasons:

- *Be efficient.* Managers and direct reports are already prepared to have a conversation about what is going well and what has room for improvement. Since it can be difficult to carve out time for this type of discussion, it makes sense to include the topic of Engagement when time has already been set aside and managers and direct reports are in the mindset of having an open dialogue.
- *Goal-set and track.* Future performance goals should be established and agreed upon during reviews. Engagement goals can easily be set at this point as well. Having the timelines of performance reviews and Engagement goals coincide makes them easier to track overall.
- *Build interest and excitement around performance evaluations.* All too often, performance evaluations are seen by employees as just another hoop to jump through. Evaluations can certainly be perceived by employees as a useless structure if they do not see any positive changes as a result. Including Engagement in performance

evaluations is an excellent way to add interest for employees by discussing topics that matter to them. It also sends a positive message to employees by showing that management cares about their Engagement and wants to help bridge the gaps.

To make employees feel comfortable talking about their Engagement, managers should explain how everyone has certain conditions that build their Engagement, and other conditions that detract from it. Just like any other personal preference, Engagement is different for everyone. If your friend offered you the same candy at lunch every day because he thought you liked it, even though you didn't, would you eat it every day because you want to please him, or would you eventually tell him "no thanks"? Rather than pretending you like things you actually don't care for, it makes more sense to be open with your feelings. People easily see how this is true outside the workplace, but often lose the connection while on the job.

It is important to acknowledge the titanic difference between sharing personal preferences and complaining. Employees might be hesitant to voice their opinion because they do not want to come across as being unappreciative or negative. Managers should anticipate this concern and preemptively address it. To set an example, managers can share personal stories of what is meaningful to them, especially situations in the past where they were ambivalent about their job or employer, and how they overcame it.

When employees share their feelings on what is affecting their Engagement, managers should ask specifically what could be done to improve each situation. Certain items may be extremely simple changes that can happen right away, which we refer to as "Quick Wins." Other items may be much more complicated to act on. With other items it may not be possible to make any changes at all. Whatever the situation, managers should address each concern and tell employees they will do their best to help make the desired improvements.

As a manager, however, it is extremely important not to make promises you can't keep. As one example, if an employee wants more vegetarian options in the building cafeteria on Fridays during Lent, a manager shouldn't assume this wouldn't be a problem and tell the employee it can be done. The manager should say he or she will look into the possibility of offering more meatless choices and suggest a potential compromise that would be more easily attainable, just in case the most desirable option for the employee is not an option. Perhaps the manager could help organize company-wide delivery on Fridays from a local restaurant that offers vegetarian options. Employees would still pay for their own lunches, but the company could cover delivery charges, and the manager could place the order.

While matters like these may seem trivial compared to the big picture, I can assure you, they are not. When managers go out of their way to address employees' concerns, staff members get the message that they are valued parts of the team. This feeling of being cared about will be returned by employees in their work and commitment to the organization.

Step 5: Develop Specific Action Plans and Goals

Have you ever noticed how things you are going to do "someday" or "one day" never get done? That is because such "days" aren't days of the week. When you fail to commit to accomplishing a task or goal within a certain timeframe, you will likely fail to do it at all. This is where most organizations drop the ball, and is a major contributor to why only 33 percent of employees believe that surveys result in change.[4] Edward

Young, an eighteenth-century English poet, had it right when he said, *"Procrastination is the thief of time."*

In addition, oftentimes, the longer you give yourself to accomplish a task, the more likely you are to forget about it or change your mind about doing it in the first place. I truly believe that is why New Year's resolutions have such a high rate of failure. Why start on something now if you have 365 days to do it? Or 203 days? Or 57 days? All of those deadlines sound so far in the future that it is easy to delay taking action day after day. When you get down to the bitter end, it is easy to start reassessing whether you would rather just give up on your goal for good. After all, you have gone this long without doing it and the world hasn't crumbled around you. However, when it comes to Employee Engagement, even the little things make a difference, and you must have a plan.

If employees have many ideas for improvements, it should be considered a good thing, especially since it provides the organization numerous options for increasing Engagement. Employees should prioritize the changes that would be most influential to their Engagement to ensure their focus is going toward what would make the biggest impact. Thus, we recommend Quick Wins be acted on immediately. Immediate action demonstrates to employees that their opinions matter and management is *listening* and dedicated to making improvements.

Your thoughts are only good if you act on them. The key to achieving goals is both holding yourself accountable and working on goals regularly. Large tasks seem less daunting when you allow yourself to make frequent baby steps rather than one giant leap. Set yourself up for success by anticipating gradual progress over time. Create a timeline and put it in writing. It has been proven that those who write out their goals achieve significantly more than those who do not write out their goals. In addition, those who share their goals with others on a regular basis have the highest rate of successful completion because of public accountability.[5]

Engagement initiatives are often seen as "extra" work for managers. Instead of this perspective, managers should schedule Engagement into their regular tasks, just like any other meaningful or profound endeavor.

Step 6: Follow Through and Assess Progress

This step is where most managers and organizations drop the ball. It is easy to say you are going to do something, but it is considerably more work to actually do it. Managers and employees must hold themselves accountable for following through with carrying out the plans and actions that were previously determined to be valuable. Managers should schedule regular check-in meetings with employees to discuss progress. When a meeting is on the horizon, people are much more likely to take action so it doesn't seem like they haven't made an effort. People can plan all day long, but if those plans never become a tangible reality, all of the previous work is rendered useless.

Progress on action plans can be part of managers' performance reviews and bonus structures to drive home the importance of such initiatives. Our clients have seen vast improvement in follow-through efforts when managers are held accountable by their supervisors for making progress on direct reports' action plans.

Step 7: Make Employees Aware of Your Efforts to Build Engagement and a Magnetic Culture

When employees fully understand the efforts their employer and manager make to create a Magnetic Culture and great working environment, employees will be more likely to reciprocate the efforts by taking ownership of their Engagement. It can be common for employees to take certain workplace benefits for granted simply by failing to consider the effort made by their employer. When employees only hear about the end result of new initiatives, such as an upgraded benefits plan or a more flexible work from home policy, they might not necessarily contemplate how these changes came about. As a result, employees can be less grateful for the various workplace benefits they receive, as well as less appreciative of their employer or manager. Thus, it is important for employees to be made aware of the significance of organizational efforts to benefit employees.

The saddest situation as it plays out in response to receiving employee feedback vis-à-vis an Employee Engagement Survey is when a manager steps up to the plate and makes real changes, but does not communicate those changes to employees. The process fails to go full circle because employees were never informed of how their employer went above and beyond to support them, and an opportunity for Engagement is missed.

A great way to show employees that their feedback has been taken into account is by using reminder "stamps" to brand all changes that were a result of an Employee Engagement

Figure 2.2 Internal Marketing of Engagement Initiatives

Survey. These images can be added to internal communications, such as e-mails, memos, and even signs around the workplace.

Recognizing Talent: Miss Betty's Story

She is more than just a greeter to patients and guests at Ochsner Health System in New Orleans, Louisiana; she is *Miss Betty,* an always smiling, forever cheerful, burst of positivity and enthusiasm. The Louisiana hospital group first recognized Miss Betty's positive attitude and ability to connect with patients and their families when she started working as a housekeeper 30 years ago. She excelled in that position for many years, but Senior Leaders thought her people skills could be better utilized. They speculated Miss Betty could make a far greater impact on patients and guests as a greeter than as a housekeeper. In 2010, they proposed a switch in her role. Miss Betty was absolutely delighted by the idea, especially since her favorite part about working for Ochsner is interacting with people.

As a greeter for the Jefferson Highway campus, Miss Betty is the first point of contact for guests entering the hospital through the parking garage. She shapes the patient experience early by helping provide detailed directions for navigating the large hospital. She learns and remembers people's names and never stops smiling. Many Ochsner guests actually stop to hug Miss Betty when they are coming and going because she has developed such a caring relationship with them. Miss Betty's colleagues frequently overhear guests talking about how wonderful she is, and how she is "perfect" for her job. When asked why she is always in such a good mood, Miss Betty responds that she simply loves what she does. She thinks people are interesting, and she enjoys getting to know them through her position.

Senior Leaders at Ochsner should be credited for recognizing talent and understanding the best way to utilize it. By empowering Miss Betty to do what she does best, she is now an ambassador of service excellence and one of the many reasons Ochsner is a hospital of choice.

Step 8: Lead by Example

As an employer and/or manager, you must set the example for acknowledging and supporting Engagement. Since functional relationships are a two-way street, managers can start out on the right foot with employees by showing they care about their Engagement. By connecting with employees to understand and act on their needs and preferences, managers show their commitment to employees. In turn, this leads employees to commit to their Engagement as well. Leading by example is truly the only way to foster an environment of joint ownership of Engagement.

The Numbers Don't Lie

The eight aforementioned steps are essential for creating a Magnetic Culture that supports the joint ownership of Engagement. The numbers don't lie; 73 percent of workers are not currently actively engaged. This is a wake-up call for organizations, regardless of industry or size, to develop ongoing strategies to create engaged workplaces and continually seek employee feedback to measure levels of Engagement and affect positive change.

Chapter 3

THE TOP 10 ENGAGEMENT DRIVERS

An empowered organization is one in which individuals have the knowledge, skill, desire, and opportunity to personally succeed in a way that leads to collective organizational success.

—STEPHEN R. COVEY

Some senior managers have a particularly difficult time grasping the exact importance of investing in Employee Engagement. In the business world, everything is about numbers and metrics. Before investing, management wants to be able to measure the ROE: Return on Engagement®.

Luckily, it turns out measuring Engagement is more of a science than an art form. From decades of Talent Management research and analysis of millions of employee survey responses, HR Solutions' Research Institute has found 10 factors most closely linked to Employee Engagement. These items are the Key Drivers of Employee Engagement, the DNA of what comprises a Magnetic Culture. These Key Drivers, in order of importance, are:

1. Recognition
2. Career Development

3. Direct Supervisor/Manager Leadership Abilities
4. Strategy and Mission—especially the freedom and autonomy to succeed and contribute to an organization's success
5. Job Content—the ability to do what I do best
6. Senior Management's Relationship with Employees
7. Open and Effective Communication
8. Coworker Satisfaction/Cooperation—the unsung hero of retention
9. Availability of Resources to Perform the Job Effectively
10. Organizational Culture and Core/Shared Values—diversity awareness and inclusion, corporate social responsibility, work/life balance, workplace flexibility, and so on.

These Key Drivers were found through a correlation analysis to have the greatest impact on Employee Engagement levels. We use a Pearson correlation to determine our Key Drivers of Employee Engagement. The correlation is represented by r and is calculated by dividing the covariance of two variables by the product of their standard deviations.

We utilize R^2 to represent the degree to which items can be used to explain Employee Engagement ratings. Statistically, the values represent the change in R^2, or a measure of the amount that each Key Driver adds to the variance of Employee Engagement. In a nutshell, this means we measure how Engagement Drivers *build* on one another. HR Solutions' Research Institute has found that 10 Key Drivers of Engagement account for 84 percent of the variance in the correlation model ($R^2 = 84\%$), meaning 84 percent of Engagement can be attributed to these 10 factors.[1] Focusing change efforts on these items will have the greatest influence on Employee Engagement.

Key Driver 1: Recognition

"Nice work!" "Excellent job!" "Great effort!" "A+!!"

Many people remember seeing these encouraging comments written on the top of their elementary school homework assignments. The friendly green ink and the accompanying colorful stickers always seemed to bring a smile to an ordinary moment during the day. Teachers make these comments to build their students' self-esteem, and to show that their hard work is noticed and appreciated. In turn, children take these words to heart, soaking up the praise and reveling in a sense of accomplishment.

It turns out an individual's need to be recognized does not change all that much as he or she gets older. Some might find it surprising that Recognition surpasses many other important motivational factors, such as adequate training, relationships with co-workers, physical working environment, and career growth. What might be most surprising is that an employee's feelings about the Recognition she receives accounts for *56 percent* of the variance in her level of Engagement. These results illuminate that even as adults, people still want to feel appreciated for a job well done.

To motivation expert and best-selling author Dan Pink, our findings boil down to the desire for feedback on work performance. "Much of peoples' lives are rich and lush with feedback, but the workplace is a feedback desert," he told me.[2]

I couldn't agree more. Sometimes managers are under the impression that employees think "no news is good news," but this is certainly not the case. By and large, people try to do a good job at work. When they do, they feel it is nice to be recognized.

The Psychology of Recognition

Abraham Maslow (1908–1970) was an influential psychologist who identified the different levels of basic human needs and founded *humanistic psychology*. Maslow believed that all people have a strong desire to reach their full potential, called "self-actualization." To reach this level, shown in Figure 3.1 as the top part of the pyramid, a person must have a strong foundation of the hierarchy of needs that enable the achievement of full potential. One of these needs is *esteem*, which includes self-confidence, self-respect, and respect from others.

The need for esteem must be satisfied in the workplace to have Engagement. If this need is not satisfied, a person can become frustrated, and feel inferior, weak, helpless, and even worthless.

Tapping into Recognition as an Engagement Driver seems simple enough, yet research has shown that many

Figure 3.1 Maslow's Hierarchy of Needs

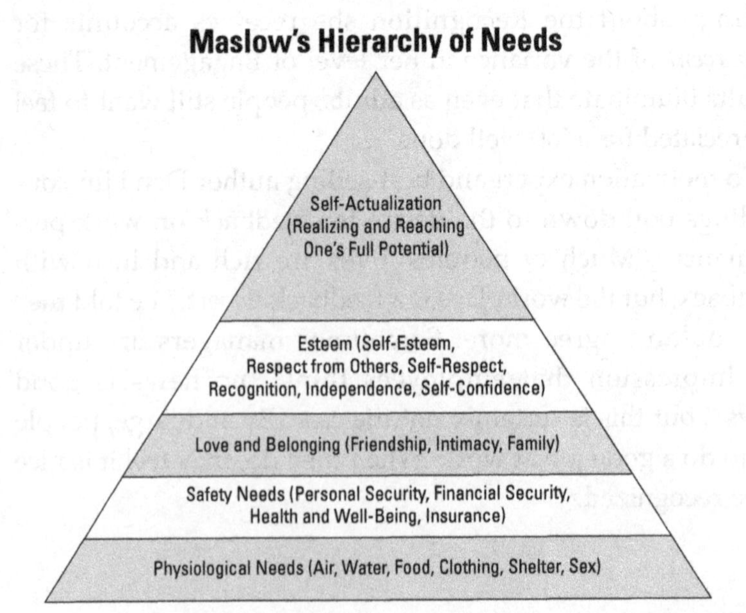

organizations' efforts have been ineffective in this regard. Only 59 percent of employees say their supervisor lets them know when they have done a good job,[3] revealing that many employees do not feel as though their managers acknowledge their accomplishments. Surely more than 59 percent of managers appreciate when their employees have done a good job, so there must be a common disconnect somewhere in the process of *showing* Recognition.

It is important for managers to consider their employees' perceptions of *receiving* Recognition, and how this can differ from their own perception of *giving* Recognition. Although managers may think they are frequently recognizing employees, many employees may not feel the same way. Numerous studies have shown Millennials like to be recognized many times each day. To some tenured employees, such positive reenforcement may come across as an indulgent and unrealistic expectation. While that belief might have been considered true many years ago, American culture has shifted dramatically over the years, causing workforce culture to change as well. For instance, Millennials are famous for growing up in an era where thirteenth-place ribbons actually exist. To attract and engage this new generation, company Recognition efforts must keep up with the times.

Although recognizing employees seems fairly straightforward, there is more structure and planning that goes into a successful Recognition program than many people might realize. It is great to tell people they have done a good job; however, it makes a difference *what* they are recognized for, *how* they are recognized, and *how often* they are recognized. Creating a program that appropriately caters to all of these aspects can be challenging, but certainly worth the time and resources. Although employees no longer need smiley-face stickers on returned assignments, they do need Recognition for a job well done.[4]

Key Driver 2: Career Development

> *Right now, this is a job. If I advance any higher, this would be my career. And if this were my career, I'd have to throw myself in front of a train.*
>
> —JIM HALPERT, THE TV SHOW *The Office*

Career Development opportunities are an essential part of Employee Engagement. If people's desire to make advancement in their own career is not fulfilled, they will begin looking for work elsewhere. Opportunities to move up the career ladder often come down to availability of open positions—waiting for someone to die or retire to move up in the company is a sad reality for many people. When promotions seem like a waiting game to employees, organizations are at risk of turnover.

Organizational hierarchies are steadily shifting from a *pyramid structure* to a *flat structure*. When I was entering the workforce 29 years ago, the most common organizational charts showed a few people at the top and steadily more middle managers all the way down to the lowest level. It seemed like everyone managed someone else. In recent years, the trend has been to eliminate middle management positions in order to create a structure of fewer managers. In fact, the average number of middle-level positions in an organization's hierarchy has decreased by 25 percent from 1986 to 2006.[5] What was once the corporate ladder is now the *corporate lattice*, with more opportunities for employees to "move up" by actually moving laterally. See Figure 3.2.

A flat organizational structure has its pluses and minuses. While the structure may be a benefit to organizational processes overall, it is important to examine how it affects employees. Having fewer managers can be good for employees because it allows more freedom and autonomy. It can also help increase workflow and speed up the decision-making process,

Figure 3.2 The Corporate Lattice

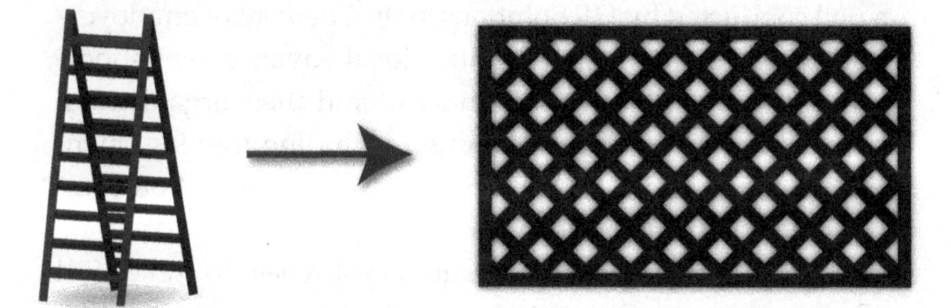

as projects do not have to be approved by so many individuals in the management hierarchy. However, employees may consider a flat organizational structure as simply offering limited opportunities for career advancement.

When managing others is not a common job duty, employees can perceive it as limiting to their career. Since so many organizations still have a pyramid structure, the experience of managing others is often an essential professional skill. If employees cannot obtain management skills at their current organization, it could be limiting to their career growth should they ever choose to leave the organization. After all, if two people have the same qualifications, except one has management experience and one does not, the person with management experience will likely have a comparative advantage in the job market. Organizations with a flat structure are generally not providing this advantage and oftentimes do not recognize how this might be limiting to their Engagement with employees.

Thankfully, there are workarounds for offering management opportunities (and, subsequently, Career Development opportunities) in a flat organizational structure. Currently, many organizations offer their employees the chance to gain more education in their field on the company's dime. According to a poll conducted by HR Solutions, only 6 percent of employers do not offer their employees educational advancement opportunities. Almost half of respondents said their organization offers a multitude of opportunities, including training/mentoring, certifications, continuing education, and tuition compensation, to their employees.[6]

Managers should encourage employees to take full advantage of any educational opportunities their organization offers. Gaining additional education will allow employees to stay up-to-date in their field, as well as give them the tools they need to perform better in their jobs. Additionally, taking advantage of company programs, like mentoring, will give employees guidance on the best direction to take their career as well as the knowledge they will need to get there.

When it comes to educational advancement, employers need to remember that by helping their employees grow, they will ultimately help the organization grow. Engaging in these types of programs ultimately is a win-win for all parties involved.

Key Driver 3: Direct Supervisor/Manager Leadership Abilities

> *Management is doing things right; leadership is doing the right things.*
>
> —Peter Drucker

While the saying "People don't quit jobs, they quit managers," is not the whole truth, there is well-founded validity to that concept. Employees receive more direction, guidance, support, and Recognition from their direct supervisor than from anyone else. At least, that is how it should be.

The Direct Supervisor/Manager Leadership Abilities is the most impactful Engagement Driver because Driver 1, Recognition, and Driver 2, Career Development, essentially *come from the manager* through vocal appreciation and initiating meaningful "Career Pathing" dialogues. Thus, when managers are not performing up to snuff, Drivers 1 and 2 greatly suffer as well.

Supervisors are in a key position when it comes to giving Recognition. Ultimately, they can either make this Engagement Driver work for them or against them. When employees feel recognized in the workplace, they are statistically more likely to be Engaged employees, meaning they will work harder and produce a higher quality of work. This high quality in performance reflects positively on managers, showing that their team is productive and everything is running smoothly. Even the most hard-nosed supervisors should be able to see the value in providing regular and meaningful Recognition since it is indirectly tied to revenue through Engagement.

Concern for Career Development also falls in the hands of the direct supervisor. It is critical that managers know direct reports well enough to help them get into the right roles within the organization. Managers should recognize the skill sets to which employees are naturally inclined, and find out if that corresponds to something they enjoy. People are not always the best judge of their own personal strengths and areas for improvement, so managers are in a great position to provide advice and recommendations for development. In addition, by initiating the "Career Pathing" conversation with each employee, staff will *know* their managers are in their corner, vis-à-vis career growth.

It is also important to note that just because a person has a natural talent, that does not mean he or she actually enjoys using it. If people are funneled into roles where they do not enjoy their tasks but they excel at doing them, it is likely that they will ultimately produce a lower quality of work from becoming disengaged, or they will quit. The best Talent Management results occur when passion and expertise are aligned—managers are in a role to create that symbiosis. Since managers should know what is best for the organization as well as their employees' personal desires, they should help find the right balance where the organization provides value to the employees, and the employees provide value to the organization.

Managing versus Leading

To be an effective manager, it is essential to also be an effective leader. Managing and leading are very different, and the personality qualities associated with each of them do not always come easily within one person at the same time. It takes hard work and genuine effort to create an organized and productive environment, while inspiring people to do their best.

Managing

- Upholding day-to-day organization
- Coordinating
- Problem solving
- Strategic planning
- Responding to current issues
- Working within a structure
- Maintaining stability
- Thinking logically
- Being pragmatic

Leading

- Providing vision and inspiration
- Shaping new ideas
- Building personal and meaningful relationships
- Developing new strategies

- Innovating
- Promoting change
- Envisioning the future
- Stirring people's emotions
- Holding an idealistic viewpoint
- Questioning current processes

In essence, efforts related to managing are generally easier to measure than leading. Since managing is more cut and dry, supervisors can often get stuck in the rut of only focusing on this realm and letting leadership capabilities fall by the wayside. In addition to overseeing direct reports, having a multitude of responsibilities can also cause supervisors to lose sight of developing the leadership characteristics that are crucial for effectively managing employees. This situation can be a major detractor of Engagement for direct reports. Since a supervisor's leadership skills play an essential role in the Engagement of others, managers must make being a great leader a top priority.

Supervisors with strong leadership qualities will inspire the enthusiasm employees need to reach the next level. Supervisors with weak leadership qualities can make employees feel as though they are unsupported by the organization. As such, supervisors who simply show up for work cannot expect much more from their employees.

The most magnetic leaders this world has seen are people who put their own interests after others: for example, Mahatma Gandhi, Nelson Mandela, Lech Walesa, and Mother Theresa. Their behavior of putting others first creates magnetism, drawing people in and quickly mobilizing them to their cause. While most of us will have difficulty comparing ourselves with such jaw-dropping, inspiring leaders, we can still learn from their actions. Put others before yourself and you are on the right path toward being a great leader.

Bolstering Employees' Confidence

Managers directly benefit from increasing their employees' confidence through friendly, open communication and guidance. If employees do not feel confident enough to go to their supervisors with basic questions, there likely will be many employees who are ill-informed of their job duties, which will lead to mistakes, variations in the execution of company procedures, and decreased productivity. Employees who do not think their supervisor is helpful or approachable are less likely to enjoy working for that supervisor, and more likely to be dissatisfied with their job in general.

Seventy percent of employees in all industries say their supervisor makes people in their work group feel that they are a valued and an important part of the team.[7] Going back to Maslow's pyramid (see Figure 3.1 on page 58), *belonging* is on the third tier—love and belonging—as a basic human need. Supervisors are in the position to truly impact this need by how they relate to their direct reports. While some people scoff at the importance of this type of people-centered leadership strategy, believing adults do not need to be coddled in the workplace, they would be missing out on capitalizing on a key element to being an effective leader: connecting with others.

Key Driver 4: Strategy and Mission—Especially the Freedom and Autonomy to Succeed and Contribute to the Organization's Success

Those are my principles. If you don't like them, I have others.

—Groucho Marx

Everyone wants to have a purpose. People have an innate desire to do things that ultimately lead to a desired end result.

While goals can range from winning the Nobel Peace Prize to simply leading a quiet and happy life, we strategize our actions around how to reach our goals. As we go through life, we struggle to find meaning for the things we do. This is true on both a grand scale and a small scale:

- We get an education because we hope that it will lead to a good job, happiness, and financial stability.
- We present ourselves well when we are looking for a partner, because we want to find love.
- We take care of our health so we can better enjoy a long life.
- We take care of our living space, so it is pleasant and comfortable.

All of these things require extra effort or decision making, yet we try to do them gladly because we desire the end result. In this way, our goals shape our actions. While desired end results differ greatly from person to person, it is fair to say that most of the time people don't like to do things for no reason. If we cannot find meaning in what we spend time on, we are likely to stop doing it.

If you are a parent, you know exactly what I am talking about. I don't know how many times I have asked my daughters to do something, and they respond by asking "Why?" Although sometimes I want to answer with the ever-popular but allusive "because I said so" line, I appreciate their inquisitive nature. Their response illustrates perfectly that people naturally question the purpose of their actions.

This situation is no different in the workplace. When employees are given an assignment and they truly do not know why such a task would be of value to the organization, they will be much less likely to want to do it. In addition, they probably won't give as much effort or attention to the project because they do not see it, or understand it, as being important. This is why it is essential for managers to communicate the importance of each and every role within an organization, and the job functions associated with that role.

One department that oftentimes gets the short end of the stick when it comes to involvement with Strategy and Mission is *environmental services*, more commonly referred to as the janitorial staff. Too often, these are the "invisible" workers who seem to blend into the background, no matter the setting. Many people see the same environmental services employees around their building every day, but never say hello. If they do say hello, chances are they don't know much more about the person other than his or her name, if that.

If you were an environmental services employee, how would being ignored by colleagues make you feel? Would you feel like you were really even a part of the organization, let alone connected to the overall Strategy and Mission? Most likely, you would not. This is a common Talent Management problem, and we have found most organizations' environmental services departments have considerably more unfavorable perceptions of this Strategy and Mission-related Key Driver than other departments.

One way in which we have helped our clients improve this aspect of their Talent Management is by tying the importance of environmental services to the success of the organization overall. As stated in Chapter 1, a hospital is a perfect example in which a sanitary facility can truly be the difference maker in life and death. However, in more than 1,000 hospitals where we have done consulting work, we know of no more than a handful of managers leading environmental services departments who took the time and interest to explain the profound meaning of the results of stellar janitorial work.

When managers educate employees on how their work impacts each and every patient who walks through the door, as well as enabling the organization to function, Employee Engagement undoubtedly improves. In fact, environmental services employees can have much more pride in their work when they fully understand the importance of their role. One best practice we suggest is to develop a departmental tagline that summarizes the magnitude of their job functions: "We don't just clean floors and equipment. We save lives."

This tagline can be printed on buttons, posters, and even directly on department supplies, such as mop handles. Using visible reminders of the department's connection to the success of the overall organization is a simple way to remind employees of their importance.

In addition to the need for employees to understand why their individual tasks are instrumental in the big picture, it is essential for them to understand exactly what the big picture entails. Senior leaders must not only develop this vision, but they must also *effectively* communicate it to staff. Only 64 percent of employees feel that staff members at their organization understand the Strategy and Mission. At the same time, 69 percent of employees think their organization makes it possible for employees to directly contribute to its success.[8] Considering that the desire to contribute to the organization's success is part of a top Engagement Driver, Strategy and Mission, it is clear that employees need to have a better understanding of the Strategy and Mission. When these are clearly defined, employees can align themselves with the organization's ideals.

Case Study: The Winning Formula

Senior management often has a hard time connecting employees to the organization's Strategy and Mission. Employees often don't understand the mission itself, and don't see how their day-to-day tasks add value to the organization.

Frits van Paasschen, CEO of Starwood Hotels and Resorts Worldwide, one of the world's largest hospitality corporations, understands the challenges of linking employees to an organization's Strategy and Mission. In order to truly reach employees, *"you have to establish an emotional connection for the employee,"* said van Paasschen.[9] Through this emotional connection, employees begin to sincerely care about the organization and its success.

Before joining the Starwood team, van Paasschen was the CEO of Coors Brewing Company (now MillerCoors LLC). At Coors, van Paasschen's internal employee brand was "The Winning Formula." Through this brand, employees saw the connection of their contributions to the overall success of the organization's mission and saw that they were a part of the comprehensive strategy of Coors. Employees at Coors felt they truly made up "the Winning Formula," which showed through the great outcomes they produced.

To further strengthen employees' connections to the brand and company values, van Paasschen's team hired candidates who had a natural affinity towards beer and enjoyed the product. They felt a personal connection to the organization itself, and therefore put more effort into their work to ensure that Coors saw the best possible results. This connection to Coors and their products was the magnetic touch that brought employees in to the company. To create a truly Magnetic Culture, van Paasschen's team amplified this connection, helping employees see that they genuinely cared about the organization and its success.

Case Study: AtlantiCare

One organization that makes communicating Strategy and Mission a priority is AtlantiCare, a well-respected network of hospitals and care facilities in southeastern New Jersey. With 65 locations and roughly 5,000 employees, AtlantiCare is the region's largest health care provider and a Malcolm Baldrige National Quality Award (MBNQA) winner.

Upon conducting an Employee Engagement Survey, AtlantiCare executives learned employees wanted to feel more connected to the greater good of the organization. Many employees had entered the health care industry because they wanted the opportunity to help others, and joined AtlantiCare because they wanted to be a part of an organization that was known for its positive impact on the community.

Although employees had faith AtlantiCare was on the right path, they wanted to better understand how the organization was going to get there, and what they could personally do to help. This inquisitive notion prompted the idea of developing the "AtlantiCare Strategy Map," which is carefully tucked into each employee's ID holder. This small piece of paper contains big goals for the organization overall, all the way down to each individual employee. Each Strategy Map contains AtlantiCare's list of "bests," better known to employees as the "five Bs." These five Bs are the areas in which AtlantiCare is committed to being Best-in-Class: people and workplace, customer service, quality, financial performance, and growth.

Each year, AtlantiCare makes goals for each of the five Bs. Departments brainstorm on how they can contribute to the organizational goals and create their own departmental goals to impact the greater good. Individual employees are also asked to set personal goals that tie to the big picture. Rick Lovering, Vice President of Human Resources and Organizational Development, says the Strategy Maps help connect all 5,000 employees to AtlantiCare's Strategy and Mission. He believes the program reinforces how everyone is equally important in achieving the organization's vision. Lovering says he can walk down the hall and ask any employee what she is working on, and she can clearly describe her goals and how achieving those goals will tie back to the organization's Strategy and Mission. AtlantiCare has seen a recent increase in Engagement, and involving employees in the Strategy and Mission has made a big impact.[10]

Key Driver 5: Job Content—The Ability to Do What I Do Best

> *The quality of a person's life is in direct proportion to their commitment to excellence, regardless of their chosen field of endeavor.*
>
> —VINCE LOMBARDI

Now we come to the topic of what people *actually do* during the workday. You might be surprised this driver does not place higher on the list. After all, a person's job boils down to everyday tasks, right? Well, not exactly. If 100 percent of a person's Engagement level was based on what he or she actually did each day, there would be a lot more disengaged people in the world. This point might sound discouraging, but there are a lot of tasks and duties in this world that are not particularly enjoyable, but are essential for keeping businesses running smoothly and ensuring society is productive and functional as well.

For example, think about the city workers who pick up litter from public areas.You have probably seen these workers carrying long, pointed sticks and garbage bags. Although this job duty is part of a normal workday for some employees, it is also a job that is oftentimes given as punishment to people who have broken the law. This task is commonly accepted as being so unenjoyable, we make law offenders suffer through it to teach them a lesson. For those who collect litter as part of their job, rather than fulfilling a court sentence, how do you think they view their Job Content? We wanted to know, so we decided to speak with an industry professional in the waste management industry.

Case Study: Waste Management Services

Susan Young, Director of Solid Waste and Recycling, has worked for the City of Minneapolis, Minnesota, for 20 years. She is quick to boast that her city has been ranked fifth-cleanest city in the world. Young oversees 158 direct employees as well as a very large base of contract workers. She says her employees are engaged for myriad reasons. "Expectations are very clear here. A clean city is a job done."[11]

Young's staff members enjoy the stability of an industry that will always be needed. However, Young says they earn their jobs every day, since they are one of the only cities in Minnesota that does not outsource waste management services. If they continue to be successful in providing cost-effective service for their city, their jobs will not be lost to an outside company. Job security is a major retention factor for employees, and they work hard because they feel their fate is in their own hands.

Many of Young's employees are independent workers who enjoy being in a field where "someone isn't looking over their shoulder all the time." Staff members have the autonomy to go out and do what needs to be done, and go home when they are finished. This freedom motivates employees to work hard so they can end their shifts early and have a more positive work/life balance.

Employees are motivated by their role of making Minneapolis a great place to live. They can actively see the difference their jobs make, and that evokes a sense of pride in their work. Young also wants to motivate her staff through monetary rewards, but has limited resources to do so. She gives a small cash award out of her own pocket in a drawing once a year at the annual employee event. Workers who haven't missed more than a couple of shifts that year are eligible to win. She finds this to be a great way to reward her top employees and show them she personally cares about them as people. Employees truly value working for the City of Minneapolis, and some have been on board for 30 years. The Solid Waste and Recycling Department is currently hiring, and more than 300 people have applied.

Job Content Flexibility

Job Content is an area where many employees do not feel as though they have a say in their own experience. Since many tasks simply have to be done, oftentimes, there isn't an option to remove those tasks that are less interesting or pleasant, or detractors of Engagement. With this thought in mind, Job Content is an area where employees rarely speak up about their preferences. Many people continue in the same position for months, or even years, with Job Content hindering their Engagement. Rather than voicing their feelings to see if any changes could be made, they assume the answer is to simply find a new position that would be more rewarding at another organization or even in a different industry.

From a managerial standpoint, this lack of communication creates a serious problem. Without knowing employees are unhappy with their Job Content, a manager does not get the opportunity to improve the situation before it is too late. The first time that managers might learn about an employee disliking his or her job could be when they are blindsided by a notice of resignation.

Although every organization is different, there should always be some leeway in regards to adjusting Job Content to make a more enjoyable situation for employees. For example, the Marketing Department at HR Solutions works on a wide variety of projects and tasks. Remarkably, all team members gravitate toward different types of projects. One person really loves graphic design. She has a great eye for designing marketing collateral, and she's a wiz when it comes to graphic design programs. Another person is our communications guru.

He is familiar with all of the industry publications and press contacts, and enjoys pitching stories and features. Another team member is our social media expert. He manages all of our social media platforms and makes connections that drive meaningful relationships. Yet another employee loves writing and editing. She creates content for marketing collateral and articles, and manages the team's written communication.

What is interesting about this arrangement is that these roles were defined *after* the hiring process. When these employees started at HR Solutions they all shared the same job duties, which were split up equally among them. As time went by, they each met with their department manager, Ashley Nuese, to talk about how they felt about their position. She asked each of them *specifically* what they liked most about their job, and what they would like to do more of if given the option. It became clear to her that her team members enjoyed and excelled at different things. While this could certainly be considered a stroke of good luck, it should also be mentioned that her team members all considered the same job duties to be their least favorite. Therefore, to make things fair and ensure that all team members are satisfied with their overall Job Content, the least desirable tasks are divided equally. Defining each team member's role within the department has had great outcomes for increasing Engagement and productivity. What Ashley Nuese did is a best practice for all managers: be proactive and ask your employees what they enjoy working on and what could be detracting from their Engagement.

Another great option to address concerns with Job Content is the possibility of transitioning an employee to a different role within the organization. If an employee has proven to be an asset to the company and a great cultural fit, it would make sense to try to retain that individual by adjusting his or her role. Larger organizations often have an internal transfer program in place. Offering lateral role changes can be a great answer for employees who want to continue to be a part of their organization, but are not fully engaged in their current position.

Key Driver 6: Senior Management's Relationship with Employees

Teamwork is a lot of people doing what I say.

—Executive, Virtual Software Corporation

Whether an organization has 50,000 employees or 15, the Senior Management's Relationship with Employees plays a significant role in Employee Engagement. Since senior leaders are responsible for the strategic direction of the organization, employees want to feel as though these individuals understand the strengths and challenges for employees of all levels. Senior managers are certainly busy with the day-to-day operations of the organization, but it is essential that they consistently devote time to their relationship with employees.

When employees rarely see senior managers in person, it can lead to the perception that these managers do not truly care about staff members. Although in reality this might not be further from the truth, we have seen this perception time and time again from employees. Senior leaders simply must put in "face time" and be visibly supportive of employee efforts to strengthen their relationship with staff members. In fact, not one of HR Solutions' Best-in-Class clients has low survey scores on senior manager visibility.

HR Solutions' Research Institute recently completed a study that uncovered a direct linkage in Employee Engagement Survey data between perceived senior management visibility and perceived senior management concern for employees. Analysis of our Employee Engagement Survey data across all industries showed a positive and quite distinctive correlation between scores on senior management visibility and senior management's concern for employees; in fact, we found a near-perfect correlation ($r = +0.90$) between *management visibility* favorable scores and *concern for employee* favorable scores.

A great way for senior managers to start making improvements to this Engagement Driver is to become more visible to all employees on a more frequent basis. As a method to enhance visibility, upper management, directors, and supervisors should commit to Management by Walking Around (MBWA). MBWA is a business concept, introduced in 1982 by Tom Peters, which has been used successfully at many organizations. This technique improves employee relations and at the same time, increases management's awareness of operational problems. As the groundwork for MBWA, senior managers are encouraged to informally visit their employees' work areas to exchange information, obtain suggestions, and learn about the challenges encountered by employees.

Figure 3.3 Perceived Visibility versus Perceived Concern

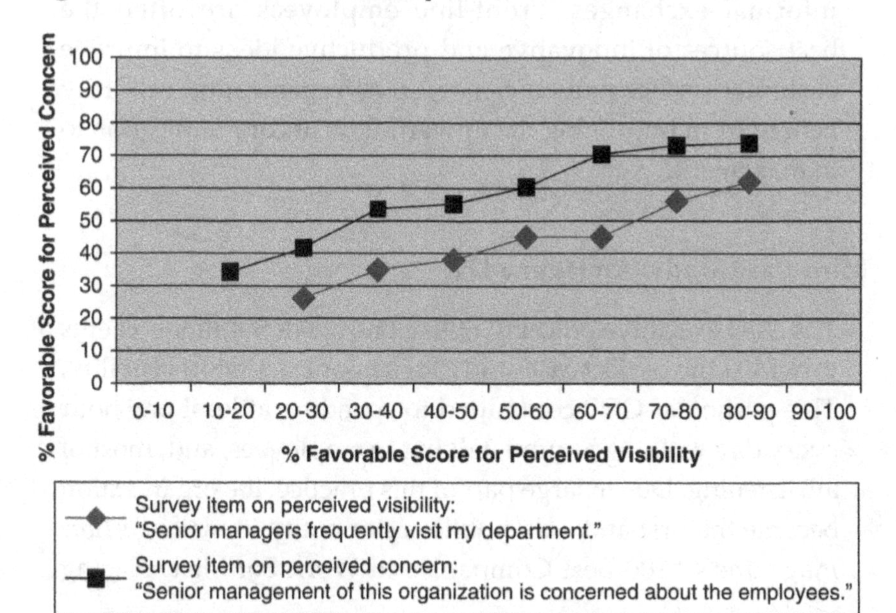

Leaders at global organizations can benefit from this strategy as well. When traveling to different company locations, senior managers should make an effort to connect with employees at all levels. It is extremely important that visibility truly goes beyond a physical visit; *authenticity* is a key component to the success of this endeavor, as it fosters trust in senior leaders. Bill George, author of *Authentic Leadership* and former CEO of Medtronic, is an expert on this topic. His book argues that when senior leaders put people and the organizational mission over financial concerns, a company will experience far greater success. I couldn't agree more. The ethic of reciprocity, or otherwise known as "the Golden Rule" provides a wonderful compass with which to navigate as authentic leaders: "Do unto others as you would have done to you." Simple but great advice that is all too many times lost in the hustle and bustle of daily work life.

Senior managers should check their egos at the door and show their genuine concern by listening and responding to ideas and concerns that employees raise during these informal exchanges. Front-line employees are often the best sources of innovative and productive ideas to improve customer service and efficiency, so an organization can truly benefit from improving the upward flow of communication to management.

Mini-Case Study: An Hour a Day

The chief executive officer (CEO) of one of HR Solutions' clients provided the perfect case study for senior leadership visibility. This particular CEO committed to spending at least one hour every day walking around, talking to employees, and, most of all, listening. Due in large part to this practice, the organization became the first and only public sector entity to make *Fortune* magazine's "100 Best Companies to Work For" list, placing

36th and beating major *über*-growth companies like Microsoft. The following year, the organization again made *Fortune*'s list, this time placing eighteenth.

By making himself regularly available to employees, this CEO helped create a sense of community, which in turn fostered Employee Engagement and reduced turnover. (The organization's turnover rate is 75 percent less than the national average.) Their organization experienced similar success when rated by its customers; Customer Satisfaction Survey results placed the organization within the top 97th percentile of all organizations surveyed.

Best Practices

Senior managers can make rounds by walking throughout the organization with an ice cream or snack cart. This is a great way to encourage employees to interact with upper management in a casual environment. Senior managers can take turns staffing the cart each month so that many different leaders are able to directly connect with employees. One of HR Solutions' clients implemented this best practice and their senior management Visibility and Concern for Employees scores quickly became Best-in-Class.

If there is an employee cafeteria or break room, senior managers should commit to taking turns eating lunch there at least once per week. They should ask employees if they may join them for lunch at their table; this fosters a greater sense of inclusion and interaction. As a case in point, the senior management team at one of HR Solutions' clients who committed to these luncheon visits experienced a 30 percent increase on their senior management Visibility scores on their subsequent survey. It is important to note that the senior managers did not establish a "senior management table" in the cafeteria, where they only interacted with one another. They made an effort to sit, eat, and converse with different groups of employees during their cafeteria visits.

To truly tap into this Engagement Driver, it is essential for senior managers to regularly devote their time to cultivating relationships with all levels of employees.

Key Driver 7: Open and Effective Communication

> *We know that communication is a problem, but the company is not going to discuss it with the employees.*
>
> —Switching Supervisor, Telecommunications Provider

Communication is its own Engagement Driver, but in reality, Communication enables the success of all other Engagement Drivers as well. Without good communication, the other Engagement Drivers would fall short. This is why Communication is one of the aforementioned three Power Dimensions (see Chapter 1).

Only 68 percent of employees believe their organization's policies are clearly communicated.[11] The greatest Communication misalignment that typically occurs in the workplace involves employees' sources of information. This Communication gap is found when considering where employees prefer to get their information and where they are actually getting their information. We offer two survey items to gauge this Communication gap, and quite a gap it is. See Figure 3.4.

There are two core things to take away from this research. First, there is a glaring discrepancy between the percentage of people who *want to hear things* from their supervisor and the percentage who are *actually receiving direct Communication* from their supervisor. Only poor managers believe in the "mushroom theory" of management: Keep employees in

Figure 3.4 Communication Gap

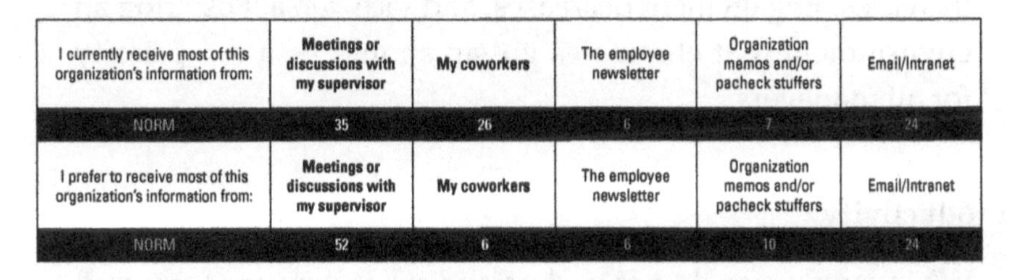

I currently receive most of this organization's information from:	Meetings or discussions with my supervisor	My coworkers	The employee newsletter	Organization memos and/or pacheck stuffers	Email/Intranet
NORM	35	26	6	7	24
I prefer to receive most of this organization's information from:	Meetings or discussions with my supervisor	My coworkers	The employee newsletter	Organization memos and/or pacheck stuffers	Email/Intranet
NORM	52	6	6	10	24

the dark and occasionally throw manure on them to ensure growth. If you are reading this book, chances are you are not of this school of thought.

A common way that caring managers often contribute to the Communication gap is due to a default reaction to immediately go back to work following an announcement made during a management meeting. Managers are generally quite busy in their jobs, and Communication takes extra time and effort. It is easy to focus on completing other tasks, rather than speaking with employees to ensure everyone's questions are answered. To bridge the Communication gap, it would be much more effective for managers to have a meeting or a quick "huddle" with their direct reports to share any news or events that affect them and their perception of the workplace.

The second point to take away from these findings (which is even more alarming) is the high percentage of employees who report their number one source of information is their coworkers. It is particularly disturbing that "the grapevine" is such a common source because employees are essentially relying upon hearsay, as opposed to factual information. Organizations that do not provide proper Communication to employees will quickly become breeding grounds for gossip, which is dangerous and toxic to Engagement. There is a direct relationship between gossip and Engagement; as gossip increases, Engagement decreases, and vice versa. Fostering an environment that eliminates gossip should be a top priority for all managers.

Productivity

When employees do not understand what they are supposed to be doing, chances are time is being wasted. Supervisors should always make sure their direct reports understand the tasks and job functions assigned to them, and they should encourage employees to ask for clarification with any questions that come up along the way. If supervisors do not seem open to answering questions, employees will likely avoid seeking answers that would help them become more productive.

Coordinating efforts between departments is often a challenge as well, especially in larger organizations. Clear Communication is vital for departments to work together in a productive manner. If employees are left in the dark about what their colleagues are working on, tasks can be missed, completed in the wrong order, or unnecessarily completed multiple times by different people. A good rule of thumb for Communication is asking for your staff's feedback. This will help guide Communication efforts for your unique population and keep everyone on the same page.

Key Driver 8: Coworker Satisfaction/Cooperation—The Unsung Hero of Retention

It's a dog-eat-dog world out there, and I'm wearing Milk Bone underwear.

—Norm Peterson, the TV show *Cheers*

Even if you don't work at the bar where everyone knows your name, some of the longest-lasting friendships are oftentimes formed in the workplace. Considering the sheer number of hours spent together on the job, this is not surprising. We spend a significant portion of our lives with coworkers, likely even more time than we spend with our family. Colleagues start out as strangers, but soon enough, they often know more about what is going on in our daily lives than our best friends outside of work.

Sharing small bits of information with coworkers can truly build a relationship over time. Many years ago when I started working at Chase Manhattan Bank as a credit auditor, I met a new colleague named Jeff Edwards. I started getting to know him through seemingly trivial facts and idiosyncrasies, such as his major in college and how he takes his coffee. From there, it progressed to learning about his family, hobbies, and sharing jokes. Jeff is one of the smartest people I have had the privilege of meeting, and I am proud to say he became a mentor to me. We got to know each other quickly through business trips all over the world, including some memorable trips to Australia and Panama. Throughout my life, I've had the opportunity to travel to 65 countries, and many of the earliest ones were with Jeff, as well as with other great, friendly, helpful coworkers. I was fond of many of my colleagues, but Jeff became one of the reasons I looked forward to going to work every day. No matter what project we were working on, it was always an enjoyable experience. I have always believed in myself, but Jeff taught me how to take that feeling to a higher level.

Eventually, Jeff left Chase to attend Harvard Business School (HBS). I was awed that he was accepted into such a prestigious program, and wished I could follow in his footsteps. Jeff told me if I wanted to go to HBS too, I should apply. At first, I thought he was simply proving the point to me that I should go after my dreams. I certainly didn't think I could actually get in, but he nudged me to be more serious about applying. To my surprise, he almost insisted I apply, and took it upon himself to help me by reviewing and providing input on my application. I was completely floored when I received the acceptance letter from HBS stating that I had been accepted. Without Jeff's encouragement, I would have missed out on a life-changing opportunity. We were able to spend one year together at HBS, and since then, we have stood up at each other's weddings, and I am the proud godfather to one of his sons.

When I look back at how Jeff and I met, the importance of coworkers to Engagement really hits home. I liked my job at the time, but my coworkers were what kept me most excited about going to work each day. I have seen this situation play out for countless employees at all kinds of organizations, oftentimes at a far greater level of intensity than I ever experienced. Many employees feel underappreciated and underpaid, they do not like their manager, and they cannot relate to the organization's Strategy and Mission. Despite all of those Engagement detractors, they continue working for the same organization because they like seeing the people they work with every day.

Coworkers are the "unheralded glue" of what makes employees come back to work, and even look forward to it.

As an employer or manager, feeding Coworker Satisfaction is in your best interest. Eighty-seven percent of employees say their coworkers are friendly and helpful.[13] Considering how positively employees respond to this survey item, employers can easily capitalize on this Engagement Driver. By allowing staff the opportunity to socialize and have fun throughout the day, organizations are able to foster employee camaraderie and Coworker Satisfaction to bolster Engagement.

Key Driver 9: Availability of Resources to Perform the Job Effectively

Excuse me, I believe you have my stapler. . .

—Milton Waddams, the movie *Office Space*

Only half of employees say they have the proper equipment to perform their job functions.[14] Half! Let that statistic resonate for a moment. That means that about 50 percent of the workforce is less productive than they could be simply because of lack of proper equipment. Does this make any sense? Unless an organization is having serious cash flow problems and is genuinely unable to make necessary purchases, there is no excuse for this all too common workplace roadblock on productivity. Let's analyze how detrimental a loss in productivity can actually be for an organization.

50 people × 10% loss in productivity = 5 people

Imagine ABC Company employs 100 people and 50 of them are 10 percent less productive due to lack of equipment. The 10 percent loss in productivity of 50 people is equivalent to the productivity of five people. The average mean income for an individual in the United States is $43,460 ($20.90/hour).[15] For simplicity's sake, let's say that is what every employee at ABC Company earns. As all employers know, employing a person actually costs an organization significantly more than that person's salary. Employers oftentimes pay a percentage of health insurance, 401(k) or profit sharing, or a pension. In addition, there is the overhead cost of the physical space for each person, including rent, utilities, and supplies. As if these costs were not enough, employers also cover the recruiting, onboarding, and training expenses for each employee. While all of these costs can differ greatly, the average amount this costs an employer is about 1.25 to 1.4 times the base salary.[16] Going with the more conservative estimate of 1.25, the actual total cost to employ each worker at ABC Company is $54,325 per year. The cost of five extra people at this amount is $271,625.

For ABC Company, this means they will waste *over a million dollars* in four years employing five people more than they would need to if they had the proper resources for their staff. Don't forget, this total was found using the conservative estimate of overhead cost per person. Considering these calculations, does it still seem like ABC Company is saving money by scrimping on equipment and supplies? Simply put, it is penny-wise and productivity-foolish.

Keep in mind that in addition to the actual root of the problem, limited productivity from lack of proper resources to perform the job effectively, employees faced with this problem will likely suffer a loss of Engagement, which decreases productivity as well.

The Compounding Effects

As another example, imagine you are an administrative assistant. You manage the conference meeting room schedule and ensure meeting attendees have hard copies of all necessary documents. This task sounds fairly straightforward, and it would be if it weren't for the finicky copy machine. It jams constantly, and you always have to open the little drawers and jiggle the levers to try to coax it into printing your documents. The ink leaks a little, so it's always risky to stand too close to it. You've ruined your favorite dress pants trying to fix a paper jam in the past, so now you work much more slowly and carefully to ensure that your clothes stay clean.

When you finally persuade the copy machine to print, it runs out of paper. Since your company never wants to spend too much on supplies, the amount of paper ordered is never quite enough, and it runs out all of the time. Last time, you thought you were being resourceful by printing on the blank side of scrap paper that was in the recycle bin. Your boss reprimanded you for this, saying that it looked unprofessional to give clients scrap paper at a meeting. Since you do not want to be reprimanded again, you have no other choice but to get in your car and make a quick run to the office supplies store to buy more paper with your own money. (You will turn in an expense report, and get reimbursed a couple of months later, if you follow up with the HR department to remind them several times.)

Finally, 45 minutes after starting this task, you are back at the office and have successfully printed the 10 sets of notes that should have taken less than five minutes to actually print. You place them in the meeting room on time, but you are frustrated, sweaty, and disheveled from literally running around trying to get equipment to work and buying supplies. You realize that now you will also need to stay late to finish your work, since you haven't accomplished anything while on your photocopy adventure. You call the babysitter and let her know you will be late getting home, which is more money out of your pocket and less time with your kids. How much do you love your job now? Are you excited and eager to return to work and face the copy machine from Hell the next morning?

In essence, the Engagement Driver of having proper Resources Available to Perform the Job Effectively is twofold: loss of productivity is bad, but when it leads to loss of Engagement, it is *really* bad. Do yourself a favor and fix the copy machine before employees start to fantasize about stealing it and taking it to an open field to smash with baseball bats, just like in the movie *Office Space*.

Case Study: The Power of the Mop

Increasing employee productivity is something that is always at the forefront of a good manager's mind. A productive workforce will complete more work in less time, leading to higher business profits and overall success. Many years ago, HR Solutions worked with a Northern Indiana casino that uncovered some serious problems related to lack of equipment. Upon reviewing data from their Employee Engagement Survey, we found a very high level of dissatisfaction in the environmental services department. As previously mentioned, this feedback is not uncommon for janitorial departments in any industry. Upon conducting feedback sessions with these casino employees, the organization's worn-out mops and substandard cleaning fluid were unanimously cited as the source of dissatisfaction and Disengagement.

Outdated supplies may not seem like a priority to some managers, but it can make a big difference to the employees who use and rely on the equipment every day to complete their job functions. Workers thought the equipment was no longer cleaning as well as it should have, which considerably slowed down their cleaning pace and limited their productivity. Employees spoke with the department manager several times about the need for new supplies, but were always told they would need to make do with what they had. Not only were employees unhappy with the resources to do their job, they perceived that the organization did not care about their productivity or the quality of their work, which was not the case.

When casino executives eventually learned the old cleaning equipment was drastically limiting the department's productivity, they decided it was in everyone's best interest to purchase new supplies. The investment in new cleaning equipment would allow employees to become much more productive, and the price of the new mops and cleaning fluid would quickly pay for itself with the increased employee output.

The situation serves as a great example of how a small monetary investment can yield a large output in productivity. Employee dissatisfaction in regards to tools and resources should always be taken seriously and considered by management.

Key Driver 10—Organizational Culture and Core/ Shared Values

> *Whatever affects one directly, affects all indirectly. I can never be what I ought to be until you are what you ought to be. This is the interrelated structure of reality.*
>
> —Martin Luther King, Jr.

Shared Values are the bricks and mortar of the Invisible Organizational Architecture mentioned in Chapter 2. Simply put, Shared Values keep you and your team anchored. I would venture to guess that the graveyard of companies like Enron, Tyco International, and Bernard L. Madoff Investment Securities LLC, show little evidence that the individuals at these organizations had (and followed) Shared Values to keep them grounded from the sordid path they chose. It is essential to not only establish strong values for employees to share, but also build framework that supports these values. The Key Driver of Core/Shared Values encompasses several different elements that play a role in Employee Engagement.

Diversity Awareness and Inclusion

As the workforce becomes increasingly more diverse, fostering an environment that supports employees of different backgrounds is absolutely essential to building a Magnetic Culture.

It is important to note that a diverse culture is not one that just employs a wide range of people; it is imperative that all people are supported equally and presented with the same opportunities. An interesting comparison HR Solutions' Research Institute found is that 78 percent of employees say diverse people (differences in race, gender, age, religion, sexual orientation, etc.) are treated fairly at their organization, but only 64 percent say diverse staff members are compensated fairly at their organization. Since perceptions of fairness are such an important factor related to Employee Engagement in general, preferential treatment is certainly seen as a toxic element to culture. (Diversity awareness and inclusion is such an important topic that Chapter 6 is dedicated to delving deeper into this subject.)

Corporate Social Responsibility

People want to feel good about contributing to their organization's success. Since employees spend a large portion of their lives helping their employer become more profitable and/or succeed, it is encouraging to know their employer is using their revenue and influence to make a positive impact in the world. When an organization's efforts align to initiatives that are meaningful to employees, a bond is formed from these shared values. This connection allows employees to feel more personally invested in their employer, which creates a strong foundation for Engagement.

Work/Life Balance

In recent years, there has been a shift from the philosophy of *"living to work"* to *"working to live."* Employees are placing greater importance on the amount of time they are able to have away from the workplace. A positive work/life balance has actually become a major influencer in not only the perception of the quality of a person's job, but the quality of her life overall. The exact amount of time people need away from the workplace varies from person to person, but as a whole, employees are demanding more time for themselves. Organizations are finding it behooves them to adjust to this need to attract and retain top talent.

Workplace Flexibility

Whether it is a doctor's appointment, caring for an aging parent, or watching a child when the babysitter has cancelled, personal responsibilities cannot always be put on the back burner. Juggling the little things that come up during the work week can be extremely challenging, especially when it induces stress from the inflexibility of one's employer. Thankfully, many organizations are offering more flexibility than in past years. However, it still might not be enough to impact Engagement. While many organizations offer flexibility in personal situations, the truth of the matter is there is still quite a bit of tension in the workplace as it relates to overall flexibility. As a next step to increasing flexibility, organizations should consider how it can enhance culture and increase Engagement.

Wait a Minute. What about Pay?

You may have noticed that pay is not on the list of the Top 10 Engagement Drivers. You may be wondering if somehow we fudged our data. I can assure you, we did not. Pay is actually *not* one of the Top 10 Engagement Drivers for employees. Do not take this to mean that offering a competitive salary is not important, because that is certainly not the case. Pay just motivates people differently than the aforementioned Key Drivers of Engagement.

To increase how favorably employees feel about compensation, managers should focus on how the Top 10 Engagement Drivers tie to pay. We will explore this topic in greater depth in Chapter 5, "Overcoming Demagnetizers: Compensation and Other Challenges for Managers."

Chapter 4

RECRUITING: THE FOUNDATION OF A MAGNETIC CULTURE

Never try to teach a pig to sing. It wastes your time, and it annoys the pig.

—George Bernard Shaw

One in 25 new employees quits on the first day.[1] Talk about a waste of time and money! A statistic like this one really makes you think about what goes wrong in the recruiting, hiring, and onboarding processes. Your first thought might be that this statistic is not actually so surprising, considering the number of unprofessional and unreliable people in the world. One out of 25 people is bound to be flakey, right? While I agree there are, of course, people who are considerably less reliable than others, the most important point is that employers thought highly enough of these people to hire them in the first place. These hiring mishaps show something went wrong in the recruiting process.

Many people think recruiting is simply selecting a candidate for the job. While selection is certainly important, it is only one part of a four-step process:

1. Finding and determining the best person for the job
2. Educating the job candidate on the position and organization *before* he or she is hired

3. Onboarding successfully
4. Ensuring the organization delivers on what it promised to the job candidate during the hiring process

To build a Magnetic Culture, it is essential that all four steps of the recruiting process are executed with both alacrity and magnetism.

Step 1: Finding and Determining the Best Person for the Job

The best person for the job is someone who has a natural disposition to be an engaged employee. While many factors affect Engagement, including the circumstances of an actual position, it is true that some people are naturally more driven than others to be engaged. These people have a positive disposition on life in general. Like true optimists, when they are given lemons, rather than complaining, they make lemonade. Though as an organization you shouldn't give your employees lemons, there are bound to be "tart" aspects of the job that are not as sweet as others. You set your organization up for success if the people you hire embody engaged tendencies, i.e., lemonade makers.

Improving the quality of hire is the first step to creating a Magnetic Culture and it is the foundation for Talent Management success. It is essential to build a staff comprised of talented, positive people with whom others *want* to work. When it comes to recruiting, people will join your company because they like who else is on board. On the flip side, having the wrong people on staff can deter candidates from joining the organization, as well as entice engaged employees to resign. For this reason, it is imperative to recognize and address when people are *not the right fit* for the organization. When you know you need to let someone go and hire a new employee, do it immediately. Managers have a tendency to procrastinate making tough Talent Management decisions, but lost time can be detrimental. The longer the wrong people stay on board, the greater likelihood they will corrupt company culture and infect those around them. Also, good managers do not stop determining if they have found the right person for the job after he or she has been hired; it is a constant assessment.

Case Study: Google

Determining cultural fit in the interview process can be extremely challenging. When organizations are very large, it can be especially difficult to define which qualities make candidates mesh with a culture of thousands of people who are, essentially, quite different.

When Google started growing at an exponential rate, Senior Leadership had a "stroke of genius" according to Russ Laraway, Director of Media & Platforms Solutions: they decided to define what it means to be "Googley." By articulating this concept, it became much easier to assess whether candidates would thrive in Google's environment.

The definition of being "Googley" includes:

- Thinking big
- Having a bias for action
- Being a good communicator
- Having the ability to work at a fast pace in small teams

By specifically defining what type of employees they were looking for, Google was able to attract *the right* candidates and build an extremely *strong* corporate culture. As Laraway pointed out to me, "We began hiring people who were often more Googley than we were!"[2]

As the company grew from 2,500 to 25,000 employees in only six years, Google's unique culture flourished, building one of the most well-known Magnetic Cultures around the world.

Character versus Skill

Of course a candidate having both excellent character and skills is ideal, but sometimes people fall a little short on one end. Which aspect is a better compromise? Do you hire the person who has years of experience executing the job duties, but seems slightly off in regards to cultural fit? Or do you hire the person whom everyone on the team loves, but will need some additional training to improve her skill set?

I would take the person with the right character any day of the week. Character is ingrained into the core being of who a person is and dictates how he or she will behave. It encompasses one's ethics, values, dedication, motivation, and outlook. It is nearly impossible to alter a person's character, for better or for worse. Skills are things that are learned. If a person has everything you are looking for as a potential employee, but he or she does not have the exact skill set desired, it would be prudent to still consider that person for the position.

Of course, as an example, if you are hiring a search engine optimization specialist and the candidate has never worked with computers, that would be too much of a stretch. However, if you want a candidate who can type 80 words per minute, you should not exclude the perfect candidate because he can only type 65 words per minute. A great personality and a high level of motivation will ultimately mean more than those 15 words per minute. A magnetic organization should offer training for employees to improve their skill set anyway. New employees' skills should be developed through training initiatives, regardless of their proficiency level. If you try to develop character in training sessions, good luck to you.

In summary: Skills can be taught, character cannot.

Job Applications

A good way to weed out unmotivated (disengaged) employees right away is to have a comprehensive job application. A disclaimer at the beginning of the application that states it will take 20 to 30 minutes to complete will dissuade unmotivated applicants from even filling out the application. In addition, a more extensive application allows for the inclusion of open-ended questions that help to assess personality, which will ultimately determine if a person is a good match for the organization. Responses on applications are also a great way to assess a candidate's writing and communication capabilities.

Interviewing for Engagement

The interview process is extremely important when considering job candidates. Punctuality and appropriate attire are a must, but hiring strategies often differ aside from those initial opportunities for candidates to disqualify themselves from the job. It is important to look deep into a person's behaviors and habits when deciding whether to hire an employee. The questions an interviewer poses can help determine a job candidate's behaviors and habits, which can assess potential Engagement levels as well. The traits an interviewer should look for in potential candidates are:

- A positive disposition
- Emotional intelligence
- Adaptability

- Passion for the work
- Drive to succeed
- Ability to accept feedback

Asking situational questions during the interview will help determine whether an employee has the right temperament and personality for the position, as well as help to illuminate whether the candidate possesses the aforementioned traits.

Emotional intelligence can be an insightful predictor of whether a candidate will be successful at your organization. According to a recent study, 46 percent of new hires "fail" within the first 18 months (i.e., were terminated, received disciplinary action, received significantly negative reviews, or left under pressure). Many of these employees' professional shortcomings are a result of low emotional intelligence; 26 percent of this population fail because they cannot accept feedback, and 23 percent fail because they are unable to understand and manage their emotions.[3] It behooves hiring managers to assess these qualities in the interview process to avoid problems down the road.

An interview is also a good time to assess a candidate's motivation level. A simple question like, *"Why are you interested in this job?"* can identify whether or not a potential employee will be motivated to perform well. If the answer is along the lines of *"I need to pay my bills"* or *"I live across the street,"* the candidate probably does not have the right motivation level for the job. If the candidate *passionately* responds, *"The job is part of my larger career plan,"* then that candidate would likely be motivated in the position. When someone is yearning for the experience as well as the paycheck, it is also much more likely she will thoroughly enjoy the position and therefore is much more likely to be an engaged employee.

Interviews are the best time to assess "nonnegotiable" qualities within candidates. Your organization should have a list of "deal breakers" that automatically disqualify a candidate from being hired. Personally, I will not hire anyone who cannot look me in the eye. Another non-negotiable quality is the inability to clearly and concisely answer a question. I also won't hire a person who will not talk about or admit his or her mistakes. If a candidate falls short in any of these non-negotiable qualities, all of our hiring managers know that person is not a good fit for the organization.

Making Mistakes

My favorite question to ask in an interview is a great behavioral measure, and it shows how willing people are to accept accountability for their mistakes. I let job candidates get comfortable and answer a series of common "softball" interview questions. Next, I ask, *"What was your biggest mistake in the workplace in the past six months?"* Quite often, this provokes a "deer in headlights" reaction on the part of the interviewee. Sadly, most interview candidates have one of two possible answers:

1. The candidate says he or she cannot think of a single mistake.
2. The candidate describes a problematic situation and promptly blames someone else.

Is it possible that I am interviewing a perfect human being? No. I am interviewing a person who either has trouble recognizing when he or she could have done something better or someone who has trouble admitting personal faults (Answer 1). Both are bad qualities, and therefore, employment deal breakers for me.

Accountability and ownership are a must-have. Hiring a person who is unwilling to recognize his or her mistakes will only lead to trouble down the road (Answer 2).

Very rarely, a job candidate will pass this test with flying colors. Two years ago, I was interviewing candidates for the open position of senior director of projects at HR Solutions, and asked this question about making mistakes to all of the interviewees. I conducted nine interviews where people gave the aforementioned responses. This baffled me, because all people make mistakes. We are human and no one is perfect. Of course, people want to paint themselves in a positive light during the interview process, but personally, I think nothing is more appealing than recognizing that the interviewee is being upfront, candid, and *honest*. Finally, on the tenth interview, I spoke with someone who possessed these traits.

I was meeting with a woman named Meredith Boza. When I asked her what her biggest mistake was, she quickly responded and said *"Well, that will be easy; I really messed this one up."* She proceeded to articulate exactly what went wrong in her last position, what measures she and her colleagues put in place to ensure it wouldn't happen again, and what she had personally learned from the situation. I immediately trusted her and hired her on the spot. She has been a vital part of our organization ever since.

Referrals

Finding elite talent often comes down to who you know. According to a recent study between LinkedIn and the Harvard Business School, employee referrals top the list as the most important source of hiring for organizations.[4] Is your organization tapping into the potential of your network?

The reason employee referrals are often so successful is because employees understand the organizational culture and can tell whether an acquaintance or friend would like working at the organization. This preliminary assessment serves as an extra screening step in the recruiting process. Employees will naturally filter out their contacts who would not necessarily enjoy working for the organization, as well as those who might not align with the organization's Strategy and Mission. Since referrals reflect back onto the current employee, people are selective about who they recommend for employment. In essence, employee referrals should be seriously considered and rewarded. If you don't already have such an employee referral program in place, with incentives, consider implementing one immediately.

While the hiring process can be a lengthy and difficult one, hiring organizations should not give in and hire candidates who do not exhibit Best-in-Class characteristics. Hiring the wrong employee is expensive, time-consuming, and can disrupt an organization's productivity for many years. When in doubt, *do not* hire.

Recruiting Myths

There are many commonly believed recruiting myths that can be detrimental in the interviewing and hiring process. It is important to recognize these beliefs, and analyze whether your organization is consciously or subconsciously letting these factors affect your decision-making process.

Myth 1
If a candidate went to ABC University or worked for XYZ Company, he must be the perfect fit for this position.

Reality
Although education and work experience can be important, this measure alone is a poor way of assessing a candidate's fit and skill set. It is also likely that top talent could be overlooked, simply because the focus is on other applicants. Do not rely solely on what looks good on paper.

Myth 2

Setting extremely narrow criteria for qualifications will help "weed out" the candidates who would not be good for the job.

Reality

Setting extremely narrow criteria can lead to a limited number of candidates to interview, which is the process in which organizations learn the most about a candidate. Overly narrow criteria can actually weed out so many people that, ultimately, top candidates are excluded and the job search lasts much longer than necessary. A more effective way of determining fit and qualifications is through behavioral interview questions.

Myth 3

The purpose of an interview is for the employer to assess the job candidate.

Reality

An interview allows the employer and job candidate to assess each other and determine whether an open position would be *mutually* beneficial. A good interview is a strong informational exchange, not a one-sided conversation.

Myth 4

An interviewee only needs to meet with one person from the organization.

Reality

While many organizations do expand their interviewing process to include multiple interviewers, this myth does hold true for certain organizations. Allowing multiple interviewers to assess different aspects of a candidate's qualifications and fit generally yields a more accurate and thorough evaluation. This methodology also provides a more thorough view of company culture for interviewees, which will help them determine whether the organization is a good fit.

Step 2: Educating the Job Candidate on the Position and Organization *before* He or She Is Hired

If a job candidate accepts an offer and shows up for work the first day but not the next day, clearly the position is not what was expected. Some blame can be given to unreliable, wishy-washy people who would be at risk to quit any new job, regardless of the quality of onboarding. However, sometimes a new job is simply not at all what hiring managers communicated in the interview process. When people come on board and see that the work situation is very different from what they expected, it is natural they could be disappointed and change their mind about wanting to be part of the organization. As a hiring manager, it is your job to ensure this miscommunication does not happen.

The first interaction a job seeker usually has with an organization is through a job description. To attract potential employees who will be engaged in that particular role, the job description should be comprehensive and accurate. It should include the anticipated work schedule, a list of job duties, and specific requirements to ensure applicants truly understand what their position would be within the company. It is also valuable to share the performance evaluation with applicants before they are hired, so that they know the criteria against which their performance will be measured. Sharing this information will inspire excellence from the beginning in achieving those criteria.

It is vital to refrain from sugarcoating information to attract talent. If employees are expected to work 70 hours a week or the job is 90 percent commission, applicants should know that up front. Including all relevant details will ensure the pool of applicants is comprised of people who are genuinely interested in the position.

Before the First Day: Best Practices

After employees are hired, but before they begin work, they generally have limited communication with their new employer. Aside from the employer possibly sending information on policies or forms that need to be signed, oftentimes there is radio silence before the actual start date. Instead of letting this window of time lapse without building the relationship, employers should use this time to make a good impression on their new hires, and even get to know them before they start. For example, sending new employees a congratulatory e-mail or e-card is a great way to welcome them to the team. To make things more personal, managers can also call their new hires directly.

Have new hires fill out a short "Getting to Know You" questionnaire that lists basic information such as where they are from, as well as fun facts such as their favorite foods and TV shows. Answers can be posted in a common area or on the company intranet, so employees can learn about new hires before they start. These basic tidbits of information can serve as icebreakers and conversation starters when the new hire starts working. On a new employee's first few days, having a more tenured employee strike up a conversation, or offer herself as a mentor, can be meaningful and welcoming. As an employer, prompting these actions is worth the effort.

Step 3: Onboarding Successfully

Despite the importance of proper onboarding, many employees are not satisfied with the orientation they receive. According to HR Solutions' Research Institute, *only 59 percent of employees believe their orientation was adequate.*

The way new employees are treated on their first day is extremely important in building a long-term relationship. As with any new relationship, first impressions count. Employees will form an opinion on what it is like to work for your company from the moment they walk in on their first day. Simple best practices can make the difference in winning them over right away. Alternately, several hiccups can send the message that you couldn't care less whether new employees stay or go.

First Day: Best Practices

- *Greet new hires.* New hires should be greeted at the door by their direct manager or supervisor. Since the direct manager should have been closely involved in the hiring process, this person should already know the new hire and can make him feel comfortable. In addition, when a manager is present the moment a new hire starts, it sends a strong message that the new employee will be supported and guided by that manager.
- *Introduce new hires to others.* New hires should be introduced to other employees as soon as possible. Some people are falsely under the impression that getting to know coworkers is more of an extracurricular activity, separate from actually being productive and engaged at work. This viewpoint is not reality. As discussed in Chapter 3, coworkers are the unsung heroes of retention. Employees who enjoy spending time with their coworkers have lower turnover rates and tend to be more Engaged because they go to work not only to do a job, but also to interact with their work friends.
- *Clean and organize new hires' workspace.* If they have their own desk, make sure the drawers are free from

the possessions and trash of the previous incumbent. New hires shouldn't feel as though they are taking over someone's role; they should feel like they are starting a new one.

- *Present a welcome basket.* A small "welcome basket" is a great way to make employees instantly feel like part of the team. Such an initiative also shows the organization's appreciation for new hires, which will keep employees on track to being Engaged and loyal to the organization. The welcome basket can be waiting at new hires' desk or workspace, or presented by a manager. Filling the basket with some of the organization's branded merchandise (baseball caps, coffee mugs, key chains, etc.) is a great way to immediately tie employees to the organization's brand. If the organization makes an inexpensive product, that product is a great fit for the welcome basket. If employees complete a new hire questionnaire that lists favorite colors or snacks, this information can be used to personalize the welcome basket as well.
- *Assign a simple project at first.* Keep it light; the first day should be celebratory and relaxed. Try not to overwhelm new employees with an "information dump" of paperwork and policies. It takes time for people to process information and let it really sink in. If too much information is thrown at people too quickly, it can be overwhelming and ineffective. It is best to assign a simple project to complete on day one, making employees feel both valued and valuable from the beginning.
- *Organize a team lunch.* If you have a staff cafeteria, just like on the first day of school, not knowing where to sit or who to eat with can cause anxiety. Consider having a team lunch on new hires' first day so they can relax and get to know people. If your organization does not have

a communal eating spot, managers or coworkers should take the initiative to invite the new hire to a group lunch.

- *Assign a job buddy.* Assign new hires "job buddies" to help provide training and mentoring. Job buddies should be star, actively engaged employees with experience in the same job function as new hires. By assigning new employees job buddies on the first day, they will feel more comfortable because they can ask questions and shadow people who are experienced. In addition, pairing new hires with employees who are enthusiastic about their work will help immediately champion a positive company culture.

How an employee is treated before and on the first day of the job can help to retain them past the first days, weeks, and months on the job.

Training

Lack of adequate training is evident to new hires right away, and it can be a top reason for immediate *voluntary* turnover. Engaged employees have a strong desire to do a good job. When an organization does not set them up for success by properly training them on *how* to do a good job, employees can quickly become frustrated and reconsider whether the job opportunity was actually the right choice.

It is essential to provide training for new hires on how to complete their job duties *before* they are expected to accomplish these tasks alone. While this concept seems like an obvious one, many organizations overlook the importance of proper training. When a new employee is hired, by nature, staff is probably very busy with a heavy workload; that is the reason a new person has been brought on board. It can be easy for staff to think that as soon as a new person starts, he or she can immediately take over the full spectrum of job duties the person in that position should ultimately manage. Unfortunately, it doesn't work like that.

People must be trained and coached on how to best complete their tasks. Proper training is important for productivity as well as simply making new employees feel comfortable in their roles. Even if someone is highly intelligent and has relevant experience, tasks and procedures vary at different organizations. Managers should not assume that just because new hires have previous experience in some of their job duties that they will not need to be fully trained in their new role. Online training modules and e-learning programs can be a great solution for training new employees without taking valuable time from busy, tenured employees.

Communication is the basis for a solid training program. Managers should foster an open dialogue with direct reports regarding their training needs, concerns, and observations. People have different learning styles that could also be a factor in training. Some employees prefer hands-on training, while others like to read instructions or watch another employee complete a project to learn how to do it. Training programs should have the flexibility to allow for adjustments based on an individual's needs. Allowing variance in training is much more effective than a blanket program, which may not be enough training for some or more than enough for others.

As a best practice, employers should seek feedback on training from new employees within the first week or two on the job. The topic should also be revisited at the 90-day mark to better assess the material taught in the beginning, and what had to be learned through trial and error. The feedback can be used to alter the existing training program.

Step 4: Ensuring the Organization Delivers on What It Promised to the Job Candidate during the Hiring Process

This is the most important step of the recruiting process. If an organization does not follow through on what it originally communicated to new employees, they will quit, and the recruiting process will have to start over again.

More than 59 percent of all employees who leave an organization do so between six months and one year after their start date. Of those who stay, another 50 percent leave before two years of employment. This means nearly 80 percent of your employees never make it beyond the two-year mark! Employees who are paid by the hour have even lower retention rates. Industries such as restaurant and retail only retain half of hourly employees longer than three months.[5] In critical financial times, the onboarding process requires greater significance. Having an effective attraction and retention action plan ensures that the people you spent countless hours recruiting and developing decide to stay with your organization well beyond the one-year mark.

Considering the sizable percentage of employees who leave within one year, the steep decline of Engagement levels from 36 percent to 17 percent after one year of service may not be so surprising. See Table 4.1. When Engagement scores suffer such a significant drop after the first year on the job, it is clear employees don't feel like they are getting what they were promised or they are not a good fit for the organization that hired them. Once the honeymoon is over, they will likely start to look for another position, particularly if they are Generation X or Millennials, the generations that have a higher tendency to "job hop."

Table 4.1 Engagement and Satisfaction Levels by Length of Service

Length of Service	Overall Job Satisfaction	Actively Engaged	Ambivalent	Actively Disengaged
All U.S. Employees	76%	27%	60%	13%
Less than 1 year	81%	36%	53%	11%
1 to 5 years	74%	17%	67%	16%
6 to 10 years	77%	19%	70%	11%
11 to 20 years	79%	20%	70%	10%
21+ years	86%	25%	69%	6%

Retaining Employees Once the Honeymoon Is Over

Organizations that experience high turnover rates often do not understand where they went wrong. An employee who was once happy, enthusiastic, and engaged for the first few months on the job can become disenchanted and disengaged in his or her position as time passes, for no detectable reason. Unfortunately, this phenomenon often mirrors the emotions people experience in marriage.

In the early stages of married life, people go through a "honeymoon phase" where faults and shortcomings are often overlooked. Rose-colored glasses filter out the less desirable aspects of the relationship, and people often experience an emotional high. However, over time, people can start to see issues they originally disregarded or didn't notice at the beginning of the marriage. Even minute imperfections can become a point of frustration as they gain strength in numbers. It can be challenging for people to look past these flaws and continue to focus on the big picture; appreciating the other party in the relationship and remembering why they chose to be with them.

The same situation holds true for employees. New hires often come on board with a positive attitude, believing the opportunity will lead to nothing but great outcomes. While their work experience will hopefully be a positive one, the reality of life is that nothing is perfect. No matter how great a fit a position is, or how much someone enjoys his or her work role, there will inevitably be points in time that are challenging for Engagement. When the honeymoon phase is over, people can let minor imperfections sink them into a rut. This is the stage when voluntary turnover becomes the greatest risk.

Even organizations that are Best-in-Class, those who score in the top 10 percent of all HR Solutions' clients, see a noticeable dip in Engagement that corresponds to tenure. See Figure 4.1. Employees who have been with their company between one

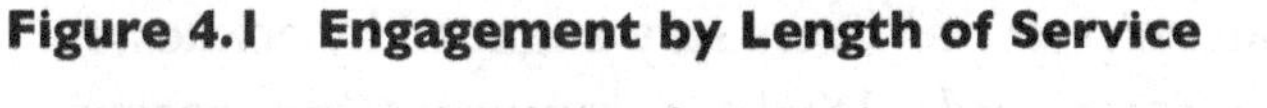

Figure 4.1 Engagement by Length of Service

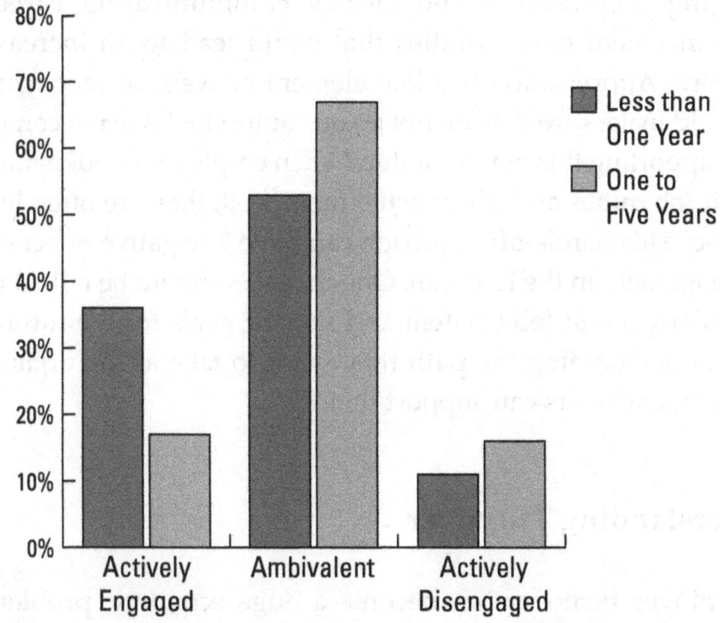

and five years have a marked decrease in Engagement that slowly builds back up after the six-year mark.[6]

We call employees of this tenure range "one-to-fivers." Managers can often overlook these employees when focusing on Employee Engagement. One-to-fivers aren't new enough to receive all the attention they once garnered, but they might not be tenured enough to enjoy all the privileges and job responsibilities for which they hope. Just like a bad case of "middle child syndrome," these employees can feel lost in the shuffle.

One-to-fivers have the lowest scores overall when it comes to the following survey items:

- *"I am satisfied that my pay reflects the effort I put into my work."*
- *"I am satisfied with the difference in pay between new and experienced employees doing the same job."*

Managers can help one-to-fivers stay engaged by acknowledging their efforts and clearly communicating career advancement opportunities that could lead to an increase in pay. Appreciation is a key element as well, so managers should make sure they do not go on "autopilot" when it comes to supporting this demographic. When employees understand their job duties and can execute them well, they are often left alone. This hands-off approach can have a negative effect on Engagement in the long run. One-to-fivers should be talked to regularly about Job Content and specific goals for the future. By understanding the path they want to take at the organization, managers can support them.

Understanding Turnover

Employee turnover has become a huge economic problem for companies, large and small. In fact, it is estimated that turnover costs organizations $5 trillion annually.[7] According to the U.S. Bureau of Labor Statistics, approximately 1.5 to 2 million employees voluntarily leave their job each month. Even in 2010, during the widespread economic malaise when jobs were scarce, millions of employees decided to part ways with their employer. In times when the economy is more prosperous, many organizations can expect even higher turnover.

Why Are People Leaving?

All organizations, regardless of size or industry, should be considering this question. If you do not know why employees are leaving, you will not know what adjustments should be made to increase retention. It is as simple as that. Many managers do not realize that the vast majority of turnover is completely avoidable. If you think you have a "turnover problem," you have actually had other problems long before employees resigned.

While some employees resign by "flipping the bird" and walking out, it is not always that easy to discern the real reasons for turnover. Oftentimes when employees resign, they give two weeks' notice and offer a general explanation behind their reason for leaving. Although there could be some truth behind their statements, they should not be relied upon for accuracy. Employees generally do not want to burn any bridges with past employers, so they have motivation to avoid disclosure of any negative feelings toward the company.

Employee Exit Surveys and Preempting Future Turnover

The best way to truly understand employees' reasons for leaving is by administering a confidential Employee Exit Survey. A quantitative assessment will serve as a system for measuring turnover through data, rather than through interviews comprised of sugar-coated responses. Employee

Exit Surveys are administered to employees who have given their resignation, ideally before they finish their last day on the job. Survey instruments should include demographic information such as tenure and location/department so employers can better analyze, and act more strategically on, the data.

Employee Exit Surveys should allow employees to choose from a list of reasons why they are resigning. Employees can often rank these items in order of importance, so employers can better understand their thought process and action plan accordingly. In addition, Employee Exit Survey data should be correlated with Employee Engagement Survey data, especially broken down into smaller demographics, such as individual department. When current employee feedback matches exiting employee feedback, it reinforces key areas for retention, as well as the areas that are in dire need for improvement. Understanding what is prompting turnover will lead to a better understanding of what will prompt future turnover. While it is easy for managers to assume they understand the reasoning behind turnover, they are often surprised by the concrete data that Employee Exit Surveys provide.

According to HR Solutions' Research Institute, 37 percent of employees have recently thought of resigning. See Figure 4.2.

"Other" is the most common response to the question, *"What are your reasons for considering resigning?"* In order for organizations to reduce turnover, it is important for them to discover the reasoning behind the response "Other." For several years, HR Solutions has been probing what the "Other" is for employees in our client focus groups. Three central themes have emerged as the "Other" reason for resignation:

Figure 4.2 Reasons for Considering Resigning

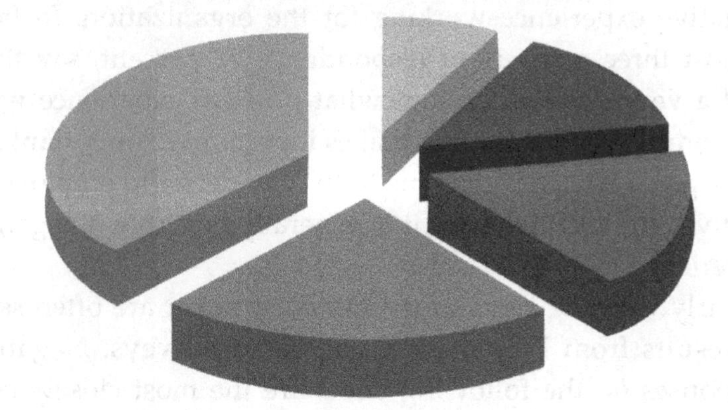
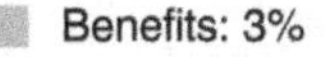

- Work/Life Balance
- Staffing versus Workload
- Job Stress

Please note that organizations' "Other" is often a combination of all three of the above reasons, as they are related. In addition, all of these factors are controllable by the employer, which makes them avoidable. Cultural adjustments can be made to eliminate employees' reasons for considering resignation; managers just need to know what areas have room for improvement. Every organization is different; that is why it is necessary to research your own population to gather information and develop a strategic retention plan.

Many employees who resign do not believe they had a negative experience working for the organization. In fact, almost three-quarters of respondents, 72 percent, say they had a very positive or somewhat positive experience with the company.[8] This finding makes it even more important for Management to take the time to fully understand employees' motives for leaving, since it is generally not from a negative experience.

Early warning signs of voluntary turnover are often seen in results from Employee Engagement Surveys. Negative responses on the following items are the most closely correlated with turnover:

- I am satisfied with my work schedule.
- I am paid fairly for the work I do.
- I received an overview of the organization's strategy, mission, culture, and philosophy.
- My job makes good use of my skills and abilities.
- I was made aware of the job performance review process.

Receiving low scores on these items should be a red flag for organizations to address concerns, so remedial action can be taken to fully engage or re-engage a valued employee. A high level of Ambivalence is also a risk factor for turnover, as ambivalent employees are much more likely to leave at the drop of a hat or for a mere one dollar more per hour.

Another commonly inaccurate assumption about turnover relates to how long employees consider resigning before they actually do so. Many people believe employees usually contemplate the decision for many months before they decide to part ways with the organization. However, the reality is actually a much shorter window of time. Forty percent of exiting employees say they thought about resigning for less than two months.[9] This data shows how important it is to take action immediately if employees start to seem disenchanted at work. Managers should not wait for the employees to pull through a phase of Ambivalence. Instead, managers should be proactive and have a meeting to discuss the employee's commitment to the organization and brainstorm ways to rebuild Engagement, one step at a time.

The Key Ingredient

Recruiting is a multifaceted process that does not end when an employee receives an offer letter. Organizations with a truly Magnetic Culture are always working to attract, and more important, retain their staff. People are the key ingredient for organizational success, and sharp and tactical recruiting is the foundation.

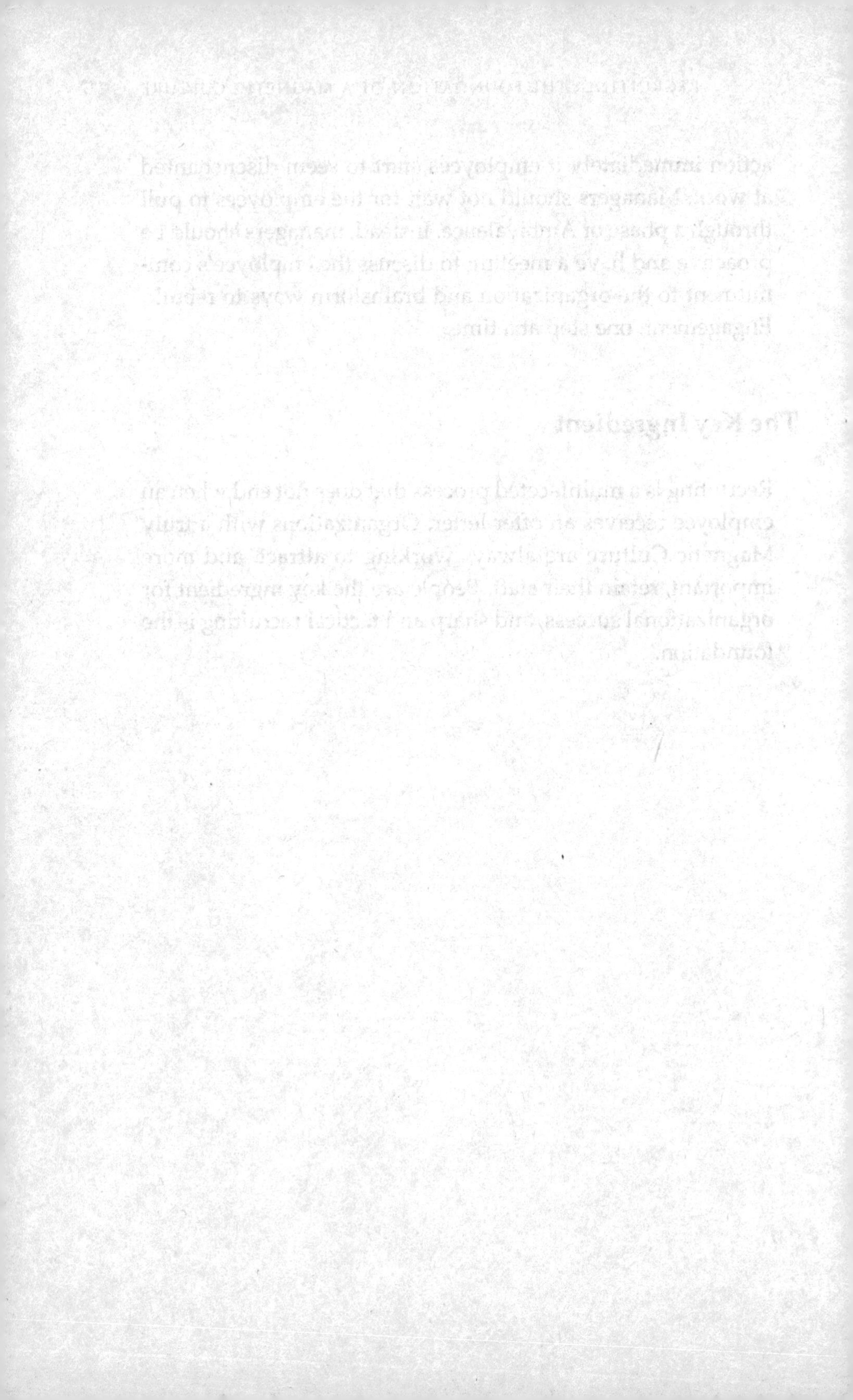

Chapter 5

OVERCOMING DEMAGNETIZERS: COMPENSATION AND OTHER CHALLENGES FOR MANAGERS

Dwight, let me explain something to you. I set the rules and you follow them. Blindly. OK? And if you have a problem with that, then you can talk to our Complaint Department. It's a trash can.

—MICHAEL SCOTT, THE TV SHOW *The Office*

Thank goodness Michael Scott is a fictional character. Enthusiasts of *The Office* love his antics, but they wouldn't want to work for him. Steve Carell plays a boss who is so clueless when it comes to management that his actions make the show seemingly far-fetched. However, through years of consulting with thousands of organizations, I can honestly say some of the plotlines on the show are more realistic than you'll want to believe.

Managers play an integral part in engaging employees. Coaching others and being partially responsible for their progress and success is no easy feat. People are complex and different. Relating to employees and connecting with them on an individual level requires hard work, dedication, and *"people skills"*—the intangible quality where so many managers fall short. Fortunately, the people skills needed to become a great manager can be broken down into logical steps and best practices that enable anyone to improve his Communication skills and increase his direct reports' Engagement levels.

As if the challenges of relating to people were not enough, the stakes of managing others can be high. Employees are, in many ways, a reflection of their manager. When employees have a stellar performance and the department is running seamlessly, it is great to be a manager. When employees have a negative disposition and produce a low quality of work, it is not as exciting to be the person in charge of such a mess. Becoming a manager is like doubling down on your employment: success will guarantee considerably higher benefits, but failure will be detrimental.

If you have purchased this book, you have probably already weighed the costs and benefits of being a manager, and decided to go for it. We applaud your leadership convictions. This chapter will help you become even better at what you do.

Industry Advantages and Challenges

Managers are constantly confronted with challenges, many of which are often a direct result of their particular industry. Depending on the industry, certain aspects of the job naturally contribute to Employee Engagement, while others can detract from Engagement if not well managed. It is essential for managers to understand advantages and challenges specific to their industry and adjust accordingly. Incorporating new best practices can make a world of difference between capitalizing on an Engagement Driver and letting it become detrimental to overall success.

We have compiled research from HR Solutions' Research Institute, revealing industry highs and lows from various survey items. These norms illustrate how managers in certain industries have smooth sailing when it comes to aspects of Employee Engagement, while others encounter more difficulties. When managers understand how their industry ties to Engagement, they can better motivate and engage their direct reports.

Each of the five survey items discussed over the next several pages are followed by a list of survey results for that item and a discussion of the significance of those responses for managers.

Survey Item 1: "My job gives me an opportunity to do the things that I do best."

All-Industry Norm: 73 percent favorable
Health Care Norm: 78 percent favorable
Manufacturing Norm: 51 percent favorable

Advantages

Health care employees respond more favorably to this survey item than employees in other industries, with 78 percent agreeing. The reason many people in the health care field chose their profession is because they get intrinsic satisfaction from caring for others. These employees feel they are natural caregivers, and they carry this identity with them both on the job and outside of work, defining who they are. When interacting with patients, health care workers are completely in their element, allowing them to act on their innate passion to do what they do best—care for others.

Challenges

Industries that do not connect on the same level with an individual's personality and identity have a much harder time capitalizing on this Engagement Driver. For example, employees in manufacturing only score 51 percent favorable, much lower on this survey item than employees in other industries. Manufacturing employees often complete the same specialized task day in and day out, especially those who work on an assembly line. The tasks are often physical, without the need for a great deal of intellectual involvement or decision making. Without the opportunity to add their own intellectual expertise into their work, and with the lack of mental stimulation, employees can start to feel as though anyone could do their job. This realization can make employees question whether they are living up to their full potential and doing their best work.

Aside from industry breakouts, one department that oftentimes scores below the curve on this topic is information technology (IT). Technology is advancing at an exponential rate, so it is difficult to keep up with the latest version of products. Since newer products have more capabilities, working with these products generally helps IT employees execute jobs to the best of their abilities. In addition, many IT professionals pride themselves on learning the ins and outs of new products. When an organization does not have the most up-to-date technology, IT employees often feel like they are *unable* to fully utilize their skill set. Managers in IT should help employees focus on mastering their skills in widely used programs, and emphasize the value in gaining such expertise.

Best Practices

In view of the response to Survey Item 1, some best practices for IT managers include the following:

- Managers should find out their employees' interests. By learning what employees like to do and what they believe they are good at, managers will be able to better provide opportunities that resonate with them on a personal level.
- Job duties should be specialized for employees whenever possible. Cross-training for various roles can also help employees recognize when they excel at a certain position and facilitate pride in their work.
- Organizations should incorporate a mentoring program for more tenured employees to coach newer colleagues. Many people enjoy teaching others and helping them advance their skills. The opportunity to help fellow employees in the workplace can increase employees' perception that an otherwise monotonous job does provide them with the ability to do what they do best.

Survey Item 2: "This organization makes an effort to help employees improve themselves."

All-Industry Norm: 64 percent favorable
Architecture and Construction Norm: 71 percent favorable
Restaurant Norm: 20 percent favorable

Advantages

Employees in architecture and construction respond the most favorably to this survey item, with 71 percent agreeing. In these industries, it is easy for employers to see an immediate improvement in their bottom line when employees improve their skills. Employees learn to better assess the needs of different projects and jobs are done more quickly and with fewer errors. Employers greatly benefit from increasing employees' skills and knowledge, so they should make developing talent a top priority.

Challenges

Restaurant industry employees have an extremely low perception of their organization making an effort to help them improve themselves, scoring only 20 percent favorable. Since this score is so much lower than any other industry, it is important to assess why this deviation is occurring. Why would managers in the restaurant industry not invest time in helping employees improve themselves? One can deduce restaurant managers must not believe the organization stands much to gain from such an initiative.

Many restaurant employees have aspirations outside of their current job and/or industry. While some people want to start their own restaurant, become a head chef, or plan large culinary events, many restaurant employees probably do not see a long-term future within their organization or industry. (These employee sentiments are further shown in high turnover rates.) In fact, many restaurant employers recognize their hosts, servers, and delivery drivers will not have long-term career plans that involve their current organization. For this reason, employers are less likely to invest in developing talent, due to the risk that their efforts could be wasted if employees resign before the organization sees a return on investment (ROI).

Alternately, many organizations do not focus on developing talent until employees are more tenured or reach a certain level within the organization. In doing so, they are missing out on engaging and retaining less-experienced workers who have high potential, but leave the organization for better development opportunities.

The fact of the matter is, Employee Engagement is worth the investment at all levels, and in all industries. Organizations that do not make developing talent a high priority are at risk for Disengagement and turnover.

Best Practices

Some best practices for managers responding to Survey Item 2 include the following:

- Managers should ask employees what skills they would like to improve. You might be surprised by what they tell you. It is best not to make any assumptions on the goals and aspirations of others, so managers should prompt the conversation with their direct reports. My personal best practice is to touch base with my direct reports once a month and find out what they learned in the past 30 days and what they would like to learn in the next 30 days. I put a reminder in my Outlook calendar to ensure I don't forget to check in regularly. I find that when you know exactly what your staff members would like to learn or gain more experience in, it is easier for you to tap into this Engagement Driver. The best practice "learning check-in" also serves as a reminder to employees that they are indeed bettering their personal job knowledge, themselves, and making *progress*.
- Provide résumé-building opportunities to engage younger workers. A summer job could turn into a position lasting several years, if the right opportunities are presented to the employee. Consider creating an internship program for students or younger workers that is only offered to employees with a minimum of one year of experience within the organization. These programs will engage ambitious, young employees who are dedicated to long-term career goals.

Survey Item 3: "I leave work often with a good feeling of accomplishment about the work I did that day."

All-Industry Norm: 71 percent favorable

Professional Services Norm: 81 percent favorable
Casino/Gaming Norm: 63 percent favorable

Advantages

Employees who work in professional services score the highest on this survey item, with 81 percent agreeing. This category encompasses organizations whose products and services are based on professional expertise rather than on unique products or services. Employees in this industry are often experts in their field who actively use their knowledge, education, and work experience all day, every day. This type of work experience evokes a sense of accomplishment in many individuals.

Challenges

It can be much more challenging for managers to instill a sense of satisfaction in job duties in industries that do not offer such an obvious and immediate "feel-good" sense of accomplishment. For example, employees in the casino/gaming industry respond only 63 percent favorably about leaving work with a good feeling of accomplishment. While it can be great to contribute to a guest hitting the jackpot or having an amazing vacation, it certainly has to be difficult to watch people lose money. In an industry where statistically most people lose, this reality likely diminishes employees' sense of accomplishment in a good day's work.

Best Practices

Some best practices for managers taking into account the results of Survey Item 3 include the following:

- Connect employees with the greater good of the organization. In the hospitality industry, employees directly contribute to guests having an enjoyable and memorable stay. Organizations should consider making a guestbook available to customers so they can share feedback on their experience, especially interactions with staff. These results should be shared directly with employees to illustrate exactly how their job duties are appreciated and make a difference. Positive feedback could also be posted on bulletin boards in employee areas or on the company intranet page, so it stays fresh in everyone's mind. Upon leaving for the day, employees should be encouraged to reflect back on all of the ways they made a difference, either by helping customers or coworkers.
- Organizations in the retail industry generally struggle with employees' sense of accomplishment as well. A great way to increase this Engagement Driver is to connect employees to organizational philanthropic initiatives. Oftentimes, retail organizations donate a percentage of sales to charity or ask customers during the checkout process if they would like to donate a small sum of money to a nonprofit organization. Managers should tally the total amount employees have helped donate to charity and communicate the totals to employees on a regular basis. Knowing that their efforts are making a difference in helping a good cause will provide employees with a good feeling of accomplishment.

Survey Item 4: "I would want to be a customer of this organization."

All-Industry Norm: 72 percent favorable

Property Management Norm: 89 percent favorable
Education Norm: 51 percent favorable

Advantages

This survey item certainly says a lot about an organization or industry overall. A positive response is a true sign that an organization is providing a quality product or service, and that employees would choose it over that of competitors. Positive feedback shows that employees want to contribute to the organization's success, which is a major sign of Engagement. The industry that scores the most favorably on this survey item is property management (real estate agents and leasing/rental organizations), at 89 percent favorable. I find this statistic interesting, since it is considerably higher than feedback from other industries.

What is it about property management organizations that lead to exceptional customer service? The score likely corresponds with employee accountability and dependence on customer satisfaction for success. Many employees in property management receive a large portion of their compensation from commission. In order to earn commission, they must make customers happy enough so that they decide to rent or buy through their organization, rather than going with a competitor. Employees are deeply motivated to go above and beyond in finding exactly what the customer wants.

In addition, many people who are property managers are the face of their own brand. You can literally see a picture of the property managers in your neighborhood by driving down the street and viewing "For Sale" signs. When people are accountable for their performance to this degree, they are more likely to provide exceptional service and do their best every time. The business model of property management naturally yields stellar customer service.

Challenges

Unfortunately, employees in the field of education respond less favorably than any other industry on whether they would want to be customers of their own organization. (In this industry, "customers" are students.) Only 53 percent of employees would want to attend school at their organization. This statistic is disheartening, considering formalized education is generally the basis for future career success. If a large percentage of the employees at an organization, or in this case in an industry overall, would not want to be a customer of their own organization, there is a serious problem that needs to be addressed.

Do not jump to conclusions by inferring the quality of teachers is the problem with education. This issue is a hot button for many people, since education deeply affects society as whole, and it has been proven that many schools have not been effective in preparing students for future success. Since teachers are the employees who are ultimately providing the service of education, they are oftentimes thrown under the bus when results are below average. Instead of looking for someone to blame, let's focus on possible opportunities for improvement. Just as when this problem occurs in any other industry, it is essential to examine whether staff members are lacking the support and/or resources they need to provide quality service, or in this case, education.

There is considerable trending for low-scoring survey items and dimensions. Employees' perceptions in the education industry are the most unfavorable on topics related to administration staff and policies, supplies and resources, organizational communication, and adequate training. Other industries and individual organizations could likely have different topics that illustrate why employees would not want to be a customer of their own organization. Strategically, it would make sense for high-level staff to action plan on these important dimensions to foster positive change.

Best Practices

In responding to the results to Survey Item 4, managers should observe the following best practices:

- Employers in all industries should make improving this employee perception a priority because an organization's most influential brand champions are its staff members. When someone provides insight on his or her employer, people take it to heart. If a friend tells you the restaurant he or she works at is not very good, are you going to go there? No. Are you going to tell others not to go there if it comes up in conversation? Probably. If employees would not want to be customers, not only does it detract from their Engagement, it's bad for business.
- When possible, allow employees to have the experience of being a customer. This will enable staff to better understand the customer's perspective and see how they could provide better customer service. For example, restaurants should allow servers to try the items on the menu for free so they can better describe the flavors to customers. Hotels should offer employee discounts to encourage staff to stay the night as hotel guests so they can experience the amenities firsthand. For business-to-business (B2B) organizations, where it would not be practical for employees to become customers, the organization can provide an "A to Z customer walk-through" that shows the entire customer experience from beginning to end. This is also a best practice for generating employee suggestions for improvements. Ask employees what would need to change to enable them to provide better customer service. This best practice is an obvious way to tackle the problem, and yet,

it is oftentimes overlooked. Employees who work directly with customers should have a very good understanding of what is going well and what could be improved upon to elevate customer satisfaction and loyalty.

- Provide the opportunity for employees to give anonymous feedback on why they would or would not want to be a customer of the organization. Managers learn the most when employees feel comfortable being candid.

Survey Item 5: "The organization gives its customers what it promises in its advertising."

All-Industry Norm: 72 percent favorable
Insurance Norm: 83 percent favorable
Banking Norm: 81 percent favorable
Telecommunications Norm: 46 percent favorable

Advantages

Survey Item 5 provides great insight on how employees feel about their organization in regards to business ethics and trust. In order for employees to align themselves with their employer's Strategy and Mission, it is essential for them to believe the organization is actually providing what it promises to customers.

It is likely reassuring to learn that insurance and banking employees respond most favorably to this item, scoring 83 percent and 81 percent favorably, respectively. There are many laws regulating exactly what financial institutions must tell customers, so this is likely a reason why employees feel so positive about their organization being transparent in service offerings. Managers in these industries have the advantage of working with employees who believe they are providing an honest product and service, which builds trust in the organization overall.

Challenges

Many people would not be too surprised to learn telecommunications employees respond less favorably on this survey item than any other industry, with only 46 percent of employees agreeing to the aforementioned statement. Consider your own personal history with cable, Internet, and phone bills—you have likely felt confused or deceived by your provider at one point in time. Telecommunications is an extremely competitive industry, with limited variance in products. To gain market share, telecommunications companies often differentiate themselves through pricing and service options. Over time, service plans have become increasingly complicated, oftentimes leading to misinterpretations by customers. While telecommunications companies may be providing the correct information for various service plans, oftentimes the messaging highlights the best features with "the catch" in fine print. Although what these companies are doing is (usually) legal, the ethics behind it can fall into a gray area.

How organizations manage the gray area of advertising ethics makes an impact on Talent Management. Good, honest employees will ultimately quit their jobs if they feel their organization is lying to customers. There is also a *very* good chance they will share their reason for resignation with their own personal network. In the end, an organization doesn't just suffer from one lost employee; it suffers from the number of potential customers and employees who now believe their organization is dishonest.

Best Practices

In view of the results of Survey Item 5, managers should observe the following best practices:

- *"Honesty is the best policy."* I am sure you have heard this before, but when it comes to employees and customers, it is certainly true. Attempting to mask the less desirable aspects of a product or service will ultimately lead to mistrust in the organization from employees and customers alike.
- Recognize when something has happened that could have led to customer or employee confusion. Owning up to a possible mistake and taking responsibility for it sends a positive message and gains the trust of others.
- Set a great example for employees by taking accountability. When an executive or manager can admit his or her own faults, an employee is much more likely to do so as well.

All industries have aspects that are an advantage for Employee Engagement, and those that are a disadvantage. By understanding the areas that will require more attention and finesse, managers can action plan to ensure the proper initiatives are in place. Now that we've looked at a number of advantages, challenges, and best practices across industries, let's explore a difficult and complex challenge that managers face in regards to employee motivation and Engagement: compensation.

Compensation

Some of you may remember the hit song from 1976, "The Pretender," where Jackson Browne sings about people who have lost sight of their dreams by pursuing legal tender and a material lifestyle instead. The supposed compromise between happiness and money is one that, unfortunately, many people feel they have to make.

Compensation can often become a driving force behind employees' motivation, or the driving force for looking for new employment opportunities. Managers are faced with the challenge of providing fair, or even generous, compensation for employees while keeping the budget on track. This balancing act is not always an easy feat. Fortunately, compensation itself is not a top Engagement Driver. How pay affects Engagement, however, goes much deeper than simply the wages earned by employees.

Pay is most carefully considered when a person is applying for a job and considering an offer. In general, people accept offers where the monetary compensation is in the ballpark of what they were hoping for. Over time, employees often expect to receive raises and/or bonuses, but these factors are not just about money. Employees want to be compensated *fairly* for their work. If they are taking on a heavier workload with more difficult projects, it is likely they would expect additional compensation for their efforts. Part of this compensation could be monetary, but oftentimes, Recognition is just as important. As described in Chapter 3, Recognition is the top Engagement driver. Keeping this in mind, a promotion that includes a title change can be just as meaningful, if not more meaningful, than an increase in salary.

In addition, a great deal of employee opinion on pay revolves around *the perception of fairness.* If employees think they work harder and produce a higher quality of work than a specific coworker, they will very likely hope to make more money than their coworker.

High performers (aka "HIPOs") are the demographic of your workforce that has a higher potential of leaving due to their views on compensation. Having weathered the storm of Disengagement where their pay was more than likely frozen or cut, this valuable population is more frustrated about their pay and merit rewards. These special individuals work hard and produce great results even when the organization falls on hard times. Naturally, they gravitate to perceptions like "Why am I busting my ass and overperforming when I am not being duly rewarded for it?" These employees know what they are worth, and if they aren't receiving it, they will consider looking elsewhere. Hence, the smart, savvy, and magnetic employers make a special effort to ensure the high performers get special attention vis-à-vis their compensation.

How Pay Affects Engagement

To better understand how pay affects Engagement, it helps to consider one's personal experiences. At some point, most people have spoken with friends or family members who were frustrated with their salary. When these people voiced their frustration, they most likely said something similar to the following:

- *"I work so hard, I bust my ass on the job, and no one even notices. I deserve more money."*
- *"My manager thinks my coworker is the Golden Child, so I bet he's making a lot more money than me for doing the same job."*
- *"I've been earning the same salary for the past four years. I don't have any opportunities to advance at this company. I'm stuck."*
- *"They just hired a new person with little experience to do the same job I am doing, and they are paying her what I make! There is no value based on experience here."*

All of these statements probably sound pretty familiar, but note how all of them involve something *other than pay*. Have you ever heard someone say something like, *"I make $42,500 a year—it is absolutely essential that I make $44,500 and I will not be happy in my position unless my salary increases by $2,000"*? In response, you might ask if he or she needed the extra money for something very specific. If not, you might ask if he or she liked the job. If your friend said yes, you could point out that *"$2,000 isn't a huge difference in salary, and there are more important aspects to a job than making a little extra money."* Of course, everyone would like a higher salary, but it is important to look at the big picture. (Those big-picture aspects are the "Top 10 Engagement Drivers," discussed in Chapter 3.)

From conducting thousands upon thousands of employee surveys, HR Solutions has benchmarking data for a wide variety of employment-related topics. It is interesting to see trending in normative scores for different survey items, as certain items tend to score much more favorably than others. In general, employees' perception of pay is only *42 percent favorable*, much lower than any other employment dimension. This is true for industries where employees make comparatively higher salaries, such as finance, as well as industries where salaries are generally lower, such as retail; this shows that pay is a point of frustration across the board.

Improving Perceptions of Pay

Monetary compensation is the last conversational taboo. At a dinner party, most people would rather choke on their meal than ask someone how much money he or she makes. Income has become more personal than a wide array of other touchy topics, such as political viewpoints, religion, and even how much a person weighs. Since nothing is generally said in social circles about compensation, people have a tendency to assume others are totally satisfied with their pay, which is oftentimes not the case. This taboo also exists in the workplace in regards to coworkers' opinions on compensation. It can be easy to *assume* others are satisfied with their pay, which could likely mean they are making comparatively more money. Again, oftentimes this is not the case. These assumptions lead to dissatisfaction in regards to fairness, which can be a powerful demagnetizer for talent.

Some people think many employees will never be satisfied with their pay because they will always want to make more, regardless of whether they earn a great deal of money. While this may be true for a small percentage of employees, the vast majority of dissatisfaction stems from communication of organizational compensation strategies and perceptions of fairness. Oftentimes, pay satisfaction *can* be improved without actually increasing pay.

Please do not take this as a suggestion to avoid paying employees a competitive salary. Paying employees fairly, or better yet, *generously*, for their qualifications and contributions is an essential part to building a Magnetic Culture. However, unless you communicate the reasoning behind compensation and the data you used to decide employee compensation, your organization is not likely to reap the full benefits of being a well-paying employer.

Pay Philosophy

Money can't buy happiness, but neither can poverty.

—Leo Rosten, writer and academic

A *pay philosophy* is an organization's standpoint on the methodology of determining monetary compensation. It shows employees the criteria considered when determining salaries, raises, and bonuses. A pay philosophy is essential for ensuring employees are paid fairly, as well as fostering an environment of trust in Senior Leadership. Unfortunately, 42 percent of employees do not understand their organization's pay philosophy. (This could be because 39 percent of organizations do not even have a written pay philosophy.[1]) To improve perceptions of pay, organizations must both define their compensation (pay) philosophy and clearly communicate it.

A common misconception is that sharing too much compensation information with employees will lead to tension in the workplace due to coworkers comparing compensation. In actuality, an organization does not have to share the dollar amount employees earned in various positions, but rather a *range* of what certain positions pay.

Organizations should also state the overall strategy for determining companywide compensation. For example, an organization's strategy could be to pay employees 10 percent more than the average salary for their position industrywide. This philosophy would become the basis for assessing compensation and determining whether the company is on the right track. By making the compensation philosophy transparent, employees will understand they are being compensated fairly for their hard work.

The first step that organizations can take to increase the transparency of their compensation programs is to share accurate market data with their employees about pay scales for similar jobs. If organizations do not provide this information to back existing programs, employees will seek data elsewhere. There are currently several popular websites that claim to provide accurate information on salary averages, but their data can actually misinform employees and contribute to inaccurate perceptions. Employers should preempt this confusion by showing employees accurate, up-to-date information about how much their peers earn in their region.

The same is true for salary increases. It is important to inform employees how their raises compare to those of peers at other organizations. For example, one of HR Solutions' local clients found that their employees were unsatisfied with the 6 percent average pay increases at their company in 2009. However, according to Hewitt Associates, the average merit increase in

Chicago for 2009 was 1.8 percent. Once employees heard what their peers were earning, they were much more satisfied with their own compensation.

Communicating that an organization plans to pay above average within its industry and region will help retain employees. However, if an organization plans to pay below average, communicating this information would most certainly have a detrimental effect on Engagement. The best option would be to elevate compensation as a method to retain top talent.

We estimate that the vast majority of chief financial officers (CFOs) have the knee-jerk reaction that raising salaries increases *total* expenses, but this is not the whole story. The true cost of turnover from employees leaving for better pay elsewhere can ultimately be more costly than offering higher, more competitive salaries. In fact, of employees who are considering resigning, 23 percent cite compensation as the reason for their impending resignation.[2] However, if it is currently simply not feasible to offer more competitive pay, organizations should focus on other benefits and rewards as part of the total compensation package. If the profit-sharing plan, 401(k), or stock options are above average, that information should certainly be highlighted.

Pay philosophy should be communicated often. Reminding employees of the compensation plan several times a year will help keep them satisfied with what they earn. Only 49 percent of employees believe they are paid fairly for the work they do.[3] This statistic could improve if employees were able to better understand how their compensation compares to that of professionals at other organizations in similar positions. Having a dialogue related to compensation with one's supervisor, on a regular basis, is critical. In addition, make sure to keep compensation plans consistent from year to year. If organizations change their pay-related strategy frequently, they run the risk of confusing their employees or causing them to lose trust in the reliability of the compensation plan. Keeping compensation programs consistent will also help to increase their transparency to employees, as they will not have to relearn the plan every year.

All of the aforementioned ideas are easy steps to change how employees view their own compensation, without actually modifying pay scales. Increasing knowledge and understanding about an organization's compensation program will help to increase satisfaction with existing programs. Even if employees do not always agree with the compensation-related Strategies, they will understand the methodology, which makes them much more likely to have higher pay satisfaction, trust in, and attraction to, the organization.

Is Your Organization Subconsciously Perpetuating the Gender Wage Gap?

Although it is common knowledge that women earn less on the dollar than men, most hiring managers would be hard-pressed to say this phenomenon is happening at their organization. If most employers do not believe their organization is perpetuating the gender wage gap, yet the wage gap continues to exist across all industries, one must deduce that employers are not recognizing when they are part of the problem.

According to the Bureau of Labor Statistics, women currently earn about 80 percent of the median weekly wage of their male counterparts in the United States. Although this percentage has increased from 60 percent in 1980, the rate at which the wage gap is closing has slowed considerably in recent years. Worldwide, gender gaps vary in size, but they are found in all of the 200+ countries where data has been recorded. The Middle East and North Africa have the largest gender gaps, while the least significant gaps can be found in

Oceania and Western Europe. Specifically, the four Nordic countries have consistently had the lowest wage gaps.[4]

While there are many factors that could play a part in gender income disparity—such as education, experience, and hours of paid labor—recent studies have shown the wage gap still exists in men and women with the same background and qualifications. In a study by the Institute for Women's Policy Research, from 1983 to 2000, the wage gap was 44 percent without equal factors, and 21 percent with equal factors.

It is essential to examine the reasons that this unethical actuality continues to exist in a society hallmarked by equal rights. From an idealistic viewpoint, one must assume this injustice is unintentional, rather than malevolent. In that vein, hiring managers should recognize the factors that contribute to determining an employee's salary and bonuses, and how gender could potentially play a role in affecting compensation.

Compensation Negotiations

One way in which compensation offers can vary among employees is through the outcomes of negotiations. While individual opinions differ on how and when negotiating is appropriate, studies have shown that men negotiate more often than women, and they also drive a harder bargain. Since negotiations often lead to higher offers, men are more likely to receive higher starting salaries as a result of simply asking for more money. According to a starting salary study of recent Carnegie Mellon University graduates with master's degrees, only 7 percent of female students attempted to negotiate initial compensation, compared with 57 percent of male students. This led to a $4,000 difference in starting salary and 7 percent higher earnings for men.

Small starting salary differences can lead to much greater earnings over time. For example, the difference between a starting salary of $100,000 and $110,000 with a standard 3 percent raise over 35 years will amount to a $30,853 difference in yearly salary at retirement. The exponential effect of small pay differences is still vast when starting at entry level. The difference between a starting salary of $25,000 and $30,000 with a standard 3 percent raise over 28 years will amount to a $361,171 difference in income over time. With this in mind, seemingly small compensation gains from negotiating can actually make a huge impact on total income over the span of one's career.

Employers must be aware of the gender differences in negotiation, and the ways in which responding to negotiations can perpetuate the wage gap. In the aforementioned study of graduate students, women reported feeling more anxious than men about negotiating, thus creating a disadvantage that is clearly shown in wage disparity. When determining compensation, it is important to keep in mind that employees should be compensated fairly for their position instead of being offered an arbitrary amount that reflects their negotiating prowess.

Best Practices

As a best practice, employers should examine their pay philosophy, and assess how salaries and bonuses at their organization differ for men and women in the same position with the same qualifications. If a disparity is uncovered, closing the gender wage gap should become a top priority. Organizations without a gender wage gap can certainly tout this information as a Talent Management strength. Making it known that staff members are compensated based on their experience rather than their gender will likely attract top talent and boost Employee Engagement. In addition, the lack of a gender wage gap shows corporate responsibility, which is a magnetic quality for attracting customers.

Although some people believe traditional gender stereotypes and role beliefs are part of the past, the reality is that they are still commonly upheld in society today. Even when people do not personally believe in such stereotypes, labor statistics show they still exist in today's culture. The only way to conquer this injustice is for organizations to take responsibility in ensuring they are providing fair compensation. When employers hold themselves accountable for analyzing a potential internal gender wage gap, progress in gender equality will be made, thereby increasing Engagement in the workplace.[5]

Does your organization have a wage gap within another demographic, such as race, disability, or national origin? You won't know for sure until you check. If a wage gap is uncovered, the organization should make it a priority to rectify the situation as soon as possible. Once it is proven that various demographics in your organization receive equal pay, publicizing that information serves as excellent public relations and enhances the magnetic attraction of top talent to your organization.

People versus Business-Focused Decisions

There is a common misconception that people-focused decisions are separate from what is best for the business. This is why Employee Engagement initiatives can be hard to sell to CEOs; they think there is a compromise in the bottom line when it comes to being concerned about employees. In reality, nothing could be further from the truth.

Many people are motivated by immediate financial outcomes. For this reason, cutting back on programs is a common way to "save money" and impact the bottom line.

While saving money in the short term is great, it can actually be detrimental to long-term success. When an organization is in a financial pinch, some of the first things to go are the "nice to have" initiatives, such as employee wellness programs, training resources, philanthropy, and even new supplies and equipment. Employees can generally get by without these, but the long-term effects of cutting back on such initiatives will have a negative affect on Employee Engagement. This dilemma is akin to the analogy of farmers and their seeds for future crops:

> A farmer has seeds for planting next year's crop, but he is hungry now. He could eat the seeds and immediately solve his problem. However, after the seeds are gone, he will be hungry again and have no way to get more food. Clearly, the smarter option is for the farmer to plant the seeds and enjoy the fruit from his labor further down the road. In doing so, instead of just having seeds, he could enjoy a wide variety of crops that resulted from an initial investment.

Thus, "saving" money up front could end up costing a lot more in the end. Which farmer will you be? One who thinks only of what is easiest in the present, or one who plans for great results in the future?

A people-focused approach that is gaining momentum is *Employee Enrichment*, a strategic approach that addresses both work and non-work factors to enhance employees' lives based on the expectation that the better a person's well-being, the better that person performs. This inspiring and effective concept was made popular by The Forum: Business Results Through People, a program affiliated with Northwestern University. While this people-first mentality sounds altruistic, it's based on the desired outcome of better employee performances. Using this approach, many organizations have found people-focused decisions *are* business-focused decisions.

Managers' Ongoing Dilemma: The Complications of Being Liked

Most people, myself included, want to be liked. When people like us, it feels good and we figure we must be doing something right. Unfortunately, this theory has its flaws when it comes to being a manager. Being liked does not necessarily mean you are doing a good job. In fact, it could mean you are doing an extraordinarily terrible job. As with any position where a person is responsible for overseeing the success of others, such as being a teacher or coach, driving people to do their best does not always equate to being well liked. Many people simply do not want to be pushed to improve themselves. These under-achievers will base how they feel about a manager on whether they are allowed to slide by. As a manager, sometimes you have to decide whether you want to help people improve themselves and benefit the organization, or whether you want to be liked.

Several years back, we had a manager at HR Solutions, who I'll refer to as "Coffee Cup Dave." Coffee Cup Dave was extremely popular with employees because of his laid-back nature and friendly demeanor. He was always available to talk about work, sports, the weather, or even just life in general. He hung around with his direct reports throughout the day, drinking cup after cup of coffee and interacting with col-leagues. I liked Coffee Cup Dave, but with all of the socializing he got very little accomplished, and the same can be said for his direct reports. He was so concerned with what people thought of him, he was unable to ensure even average quality control, hold his team accountable for their mistakes, or deliver bad news about their performance. Although he had good people in his department, they didn't produce the caliber of work they should have, because there was no accountability-based management. Great managers do not delay crucial conversations. Poor managers do. Eventually, we actually ended up losing a few large clients because of Coffee Cup Dave, and it was the nadir in HR Solutions' productivity and quality results. Dave drank coffee, had many laughs, and kept friends. HR Solutions lost clients and, temporarily, lost revenue.

The truth about being liked is that it happens *naturally* when you help people pursue their goals. If employees want to advance their skills and knowledge and you help them do it, they will like you. If employees want to laze through their day in a vegetative state, of course they are not going to like you if you try to get them to work. It's common sense. Effective managers are usually well liked by engaged employees, and even ambivalent employees. Disengaged employees are generally negative and respond poorly to supervision in general. Worrying about what this group of people thinks about you is a waste of time. Those who are not willing to give their best effort should not have a place in your organization anyway, so it certainly should not matter how much they like you. Focus on being a great leader, and being liked is a tangential benefit you will enjoy from your team.

Managing Workplace Conflicts

As a manager, encountering conflicts is inevitable. It would be phenomenal if everyone saw eye to eye 100 percent of the time, but realistically, that is not going to happen. To maintain a Magnetic Culture, it is crucial for managers to help crush the conflicts that threaten to polarize the workforce. Managers should keep their ear to the ground to help preempt issues that could become detrimental to Engagement over time.

By nature, most people try to avoid conflict. This avoidance is especially true in the workplace, where the stakes of disagreement are much higher because pleasantries and cooperation are expected. The thought of addressing conflict by confronting a colleague cannot only be worrisome, but also physiologically disturbing. The anticipation of such an event can often create a general nervous feeling that is hard to shake throughout the workday, thus damaging employees' productivity. Many people try to push thoughts of conflict away, avoiding possible culmination in what they perceive to be a confrontation. Unfortunately, oftentimes the source of conflict does not go away by itself. When left unaddressed, an employee's level of irritation can grow exponentially. What was once a minor frustration can quickly grow into a full-blown disturbance, causing a major Engagement roadblock.

A pressing challenge for managers is fostering an environment where open communication is highly valued, and conflicts are managed long before they reach a boiling point. According to *Talent Management* magazine, people will go to great lengths to avoid having unpleasant conversations in the workplace. Thirty-four percent of respondents reported avoiding a crucial conversation for over a month, while nearly one in four put off a crucial conversation for more than a year. When the conversation involved a manager, avoidance levels were even higher. Reasons for avoidance varied, but most were caused by fear of the conversation ending badly, resulting in a negative working environment.[6]

Setting an Example

Managers must set the example for conflict management through their actions. If employees view their manager as someone who does not handle conflict well, they will be apprehensive of seeking help from their manager if there is a conflict with another employee. In addition, if employees view their manager as someone with a short fuse, it is much more likely they will avoid confrontations with that manager, no matter how damaging it is in the long term. The same holds true for managers who come across as unapproachable: direct reports will not come to them with their concerns.

As a best practice, managers should try to view all conflicts through a lens of professionalism. This idea sounds simple, but it can actually be one of the hardest things a manager learns to do. Personal feelings and opinions that are not directly related to the job need to be kept in check.

A cohesive staff is generally much more productive and engaged than a staff that has interpersonal issues. The ability to help employees resolve conflict without confrontation is a valuable skill for managers in any industry. Whether it is through surveys, a suggestion box, or simply fostering a culture that encourages open communication, creating an environment where coworkers get along plays a big part in building a Magnetic Culture.[7]

Engagement in a Unionized Environment

Imagine an organization where Employee Engagement and satisfaction levels and morale have reached an all-time low. The organization's Senior Management seems unwilling to respond to the employees' need for adequate supplies, decent salary and benefits packages, and safe and secure physical working conditions. Eventually, in an attempt to increase the satisfaction level, the employees decide to form a union. The union immediately gets to work on the more pressing issues, and the organization sees an increase in satisfaction and Engagement levels. However, despite having a union in place, the organization's Employee Engagement and satisfaction levels never reach the levels of its competitors, where employees have never needed to form a union.

This scenario is actually more familiar than one might think. The United States has 16.1 million union members.[8] In the European Union, one of four employees is a union member, totaling 60 million people.[9] Employees often join unions in an attempt to increase their satisfaction level, but never hit the same satisfaction levels as their nonunionized peers. This phenomenon can be attributed to several factors.

Complicated Communication Routes

As discussed earlier in this book (see Chapter 1), Communication is one of HR Solutions' Power Dimensions, an area where Best-in-Class organizations unwaveringly score well. Good communication between management and employees is key to building both Employee Engagement and satisfaction. However, the introduction of a union complicates normal communication routes since certain messages must go through the union to get to and from employees. This additional step in communication can act as a filter and can also delay, cloud, or eradicate messages, which may lead to confusion and frustration among employees.

Focus of Union

When a union forms, its immediate focus is on contract negotiations, pay, benefits, and HR/workplace policies. While these elements are all important to employees, they are not the Key Drivers of Employee Engagement or Overall Job Satisfaction. To raise Engagement and satisfaction levels, unions would instead have to focus on issues like Recognition, Career Development, Senior Management's Relationship with Employees, and the organization's Strategy and Mission.

Negotiated Pay Increases

In unionized environments, compensation is regulated by contract. While contracts allow employees to receive fair wages, they remove the connection between merit and compensation. Recognition is the top Driver of Employee Engagement, so the removal of this connection can lead to a decrease in Engagement levels. In addition, when a union is present, employees must hand over a portion of their paycheck each month as member dues. Paying union dues can add to feelings of dissatisfaction, especially when employees do not see the results they expected from unionization.

Union Control

In a unionized environment, the union tends to determine what resources are needed and the organization's physical working conditions. This control means that when employees need new cleaning supplies or an overhead light replaced, the union has to approve the purchase or work before it is completed, which can cause interference and delay the process.

One of our gaming clients provided an excellent example of how the added step of getting union approval can delay a simple change. The employees wanted to move a slot machine two feet because it was causing issues with the flow of foot traffic. To do so, they had to fill out paperwork and have it sent through the union and the government (Canada). The entire process ended up taking two months to move the slot machine two feet.

An Us-versus-Them Mentality

The presence of a union can heighten tension between groups of employees and between employees and management because it creates an us-versus-them mentality. Employees belonging to different departments can feel this divide when they believe their respective department's needs are not being treated with the same care as other departments' needs. The presence of a union also makes employees feel even further separated from management, which can make management seem like the "enemy," cause a lack of trust in management, and lower Engagement and satisfaction levels.

Unions as an Extreme

Since most organizations with unions do not have more satisfied or engaged employees, nonunionized organizations should do everything they can to make sure their employees do not feel the need to organize. One way to ensure that an organization's employees do not want to form a union is through HR Solutions' Unionization Vulnerability Index (UVI). Our UVI is the only tool in existence that has been scientifically validated, as shown by a 92 percent success rate as defined by no card signing within five years of the initial survey.

Unionization does not tend to lead to increased Engagement or satisfaction levels, so it should only be used as a last resort for organizations with extremely low Employee Engagement and satisfaction levels. The best option for organizations is to minimize the possibility that employees will want to unionize. Smart organizations that want to remain non-union listen to their employees through formal and confidential surveying, making their union vulnerability risk nonexistent. By staying ahead of the curve and truly caring about employees, organizations can minimize their risk of unionization.[10]

Be Aware and Make an Effort

Although there are many elements that threaten to demagnetize an organization's culture, managers can actively combat these issues by simply being aware of them and making an effort. What makes people great managers is not necessarily what they know, but their interest and dedication to improvement.

In the next chapter, we'll explore a topic briefly mentioned here, diversity in the workplace, and discuss how to embrace diversity to further engage employees and magnetize your culture.

Chapter 6

DO NOT IGNORE DIVERSITY

There are only two things I can't stand in this world. People who are intolerant of other people's cultures and the Dutch.

—MICHAEL CAINE'S CHARACTER, NIGEL POWERS, IN THE AUSTIN POWERS MOVIE *Goldmember*

Diversity is an "elephant in the room" at many organizations. As globalization increases and the demographics of the workforce encompass employees with disparate backgrounds, diversity becomes a greater element than ever. Unfortunately, many organizations do not know what to do to address this change.

We are taught early in life that "what's on the inside" matters, and that it is wrong to judge people for any other factor. This early conditioning oftentimes teaches children to *ignore* differences, rather than *embrace* what makes us different. However, as we get older, we notice people *are* affected by their respective cultural experiences. Whether consciously or unconsciously, our gender, socioeconomic background, social traditions, and other experiences play a part in who we become and what we value. Unfortunately, these elements can seem like a taboo topic, especially in the workplace. When it comes to working with colleagues who are of a different background from ours, many people would consider it inappropriate to acknowledge the aforementioned differences even exist, let alone affect a person's work performance. Dusting diversity "under the rug" has essentially left many organizations with an "elephant in the room."

Recent research has uncovered a positive correlation between diversity satisfaction and overall job satisfaction. The three survey items below show that when employees rate their organization as treating both employees and customers of diverse backgrounds fairly, the organizational levels of employee satisfaction and Engagement are also more favorable. See Table 6.1.

As discussed previously, the correlation coefficient (*r*) is a value that quantifies the relationship between two variables. The value of *r* can be between +1.00 (positive correlation) and –1.00 (negative correlation). A positive correlation signifies that one variable increases as the other increases (i.e., height versus weight); therefore, a perfect correlation would yield a score of +1.00. A negative correlation, or inverse relationship, shows that as one variable becomes larger the other becomes

Table 6.1 Correlation between Employee Survey Items and Diversity Satisfaction

Employee Engagement Survey Items	Pearson Correlation
Outcome variable: overall job satisfaction	1.00
Diverse customers (differences in race, gender, age, religion, sexual orientation, etc.) are treated fairly by this organization	0.42
Diverse employees are treated fairly with regard to their career advancement by this organization	0.41
Diverse employees (differences in race, gender, age, religion, sexual orientation, etc.) are treated fairly by this organization	0.40

Figure 6.1 Job Satisfaction versus Diversity Satisfaction

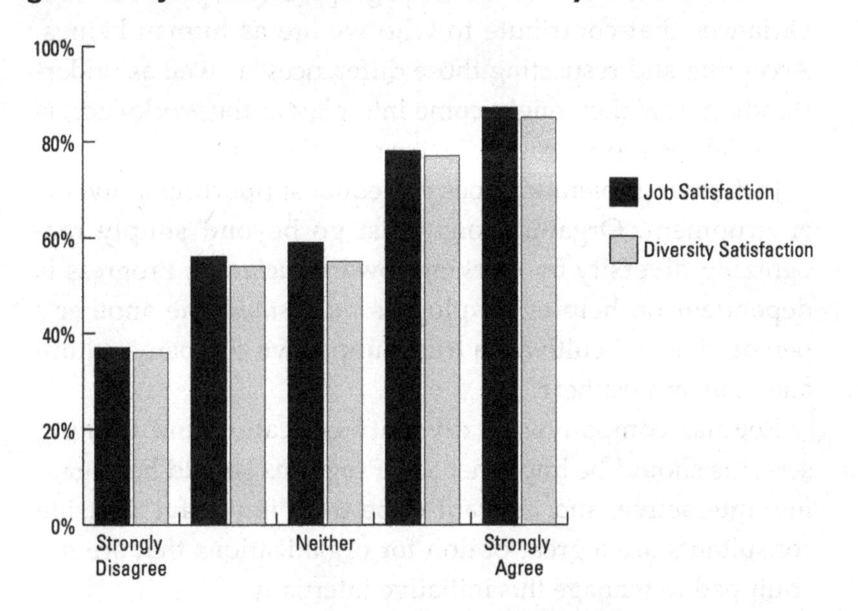

smaller (i.e., weight versus gymnastic ability); therefore, a perfect negative correlation would be –1.00. The absolute lack of a correlation, meaning there is no relationship between two variables, would yield a score of 0. Correlations do not imply causation, but rather show a relationship.

We have already discussed how Engagement affects an organization's bottom line. However, diversity satisfaction could be the missing piece of the puzzle for many organizations that have reached an Engagement plateau. See Figure 6.1.

Diversity and Organizational Policies

What is diversity? This question may seem like an obvious one but it needs to be addressed, especially since diversity is much more than the differences and similarities that meet the eye.

Diversity encompasses all demographic and philosophical variances that contribute to who we are as human beings. Accepting and respecting those differences, as well as understanding how they might come into play in the workplace, is essential for supporting a diverse organization.

Just having tolerance does not equal supporting a diverse environment. Organizations must go beyond simply recognizing diversity by working toward *inclusion*. Progress is dependent on helping employees *understand* one another's perspective and cultivate a truly supportive company culture and team atmosphere.

Regular companywide diversity education and training sessions should be implemented. Programs should be engaging, interactive, and relevant to be truly impactful. Outside consultants are a great option for organizations that are not equipped to manage this initiative internally.

Internal and organizational policies are the best place to start when assessing your organization's current stance on diversity issues. Internal audits are essential not only for Engagement but for legal compliance as well.

Religion

An area where organizations are prone to problems is religion. Title VII of the Civil Rights Act of 1964 states employers must provide reasonable accommodations for religious observations of all employees, unless doing so would cause undo hardship to the business. According to the Equal Employment Opportunity Commission (EEOC), religion-based charges have increased approximately 50 percent since 1997, and payouts have increased by about 160 percent, totaling over 10 million dollars in 2010.[1] I do not condone making fear-based decisions when it comes to shaping your business, but it is important to understand Talent Management risks and more important, *why* these laws are in place.

For many people, religion is a core part of who they are. It is something that is not up for compromise under any circumstances, including policies that are put in place by one's employer. If a person desires time off from work to observe a religious holiday, or simply time off during the day to pray, employers should accommodate those needs. While the exact rules can be debated in terms of legal compliance, from a standpoint of upholding a culture of engaged employees, allowing staff a great deal of freedom in this regard is a best practice.

Most organizations offer paid time off (PTO) for religious holidays, but those holidays are often limited to Christian holidays. Those who observe other religions may not see these PTO days as a benefit, particularly if they observe other religious holidays that are not included as PTO. A good solution is to offer floating holidays, which can be used on common religious holidays or as otherwise needed by individual employees. In 2010, 76 percent of DiversityInc Top 50 Companies for Diversity offered floating religious holidays versus 34 percent of companies nationally. In addition, 74 percent of the DiversityInc Top 50 Companies for Diversity offered on-site religious accommodations, such as prayer rooms, compared with 8 percent of companies nationally.[2]

When Ethnic "Minority" Becomes Ethnic "Majority"

Current birthrates for minorities in the United States exceed that of Caucasians. Based on U.S. Census Bureau estimates, the United States is on track to reach "Majority Minority" status by 2042, with continued growth of Asian, Black, and Hispanic populations. As ethnic diversity increases, it will become even more important for organizations to foster a culture where all employees feel welcomed and included.

Case Study: Boys and Girls Clubs of America

Known for its dedication to at-risk youth, Boys and Girls Clubs of America has changed communities across the country. With nearly 4,000 locations and a presence in all 50 states, Puerto Rico, and the Virgin Islands, the organization has been able to reach out to over four million young people.

Many of the youth that the organization serves are ethnic minorities, which brings a heightened need for diversity education and training of national staff members. Terri Dorsey, Director of Organizational Development, says Diversity and Inclusion are a top Talent Management priority. *"As an organization that serves youth, we already knew that our strategy for kids was to create a positive place that promotes a sense of competence, belonging, influence, and usefulness. We realized those principles should also drive the environment we create for our staff members."*[3]

Over the past several years, the Boys and Girls Clubs of America has increased its support for a diverse staff through numerous initiatives. Annual diversity-related training programs have helped educate employees on the importance of diversity and how to continue fostering an environment that supports inclusion. Staff members also have the opportunity to take a leadership role by managing diversity celebrations, such as Latin American Heritage Month, Black History Month, Women's History Month, and Disability Awareness. These efforts illustrate how it is essential to understand diversity at the employee level to be able to effectively reach diverse customers. *"I believe our diversity efforts, focused on creating that positive environment for everyone, have much to do with our current success,"* said Dorsey.

As workplace ethnic demographics continue to change exponentially, is your organization prepared to attract and retain diverse top talent?

Racial Disparity in Views on Diversity Efforts

When it comes to diversity efforts, success is often viewed differently by members of different races. While the majority ethnic population may be satisfied with diversity efforts, minority populations are generally less satisfied. The following benchmarking data[4] shows the differences in feedback by race:

"This organization has been effective in promoting diversity here."

- Black: 59 percent agree
- White: 78 percent agree
- Hispanic: 56 percent agree

"My supervisor shows the same level of interest in all his/her employees' careers, regardless of race, gender, age, religion, or sexual orientation."

- Black: 61 percent agree
- White: 79 percent agree
- Hispanic: 82 percent agree

"Training is needed at this organization to help employees at all levels overcome communication barriers."

- Black: 80 percent agree
- White: 60 percent agree
- Hispanic: 75 percent agree

"My coworkers treat all customers equally, regardless of race, gender, age, religion, or sexual orientation."
Black: 89 percent agree
White: 90 percent agree
Hispanic: 91 percent agree

Organizations can better assess the perceptions of their population by conducting an Employee Survey and separating responses by demographic. This data will allow Senior Leaders to understand differences in opinion, and likely, Engagement, of various ethnic populations within the organization. From there, they can action plan to address areas for improvement.

A Childhood and Lifelong Lesson in Diversity

When I was in sixth grade, I used to spend recess hiding under a truck in a tucked-away garage at the end of my elementary school's property. I would have much rather been outside playing with friends, but that was not an option. I was one of the only Caucasian students enrolled in the Native American elementary school on a reservation in northern Wisconsin, and I was regularly beaten up because of my skin color. Recess was guaranteed torture.

It started on my first day of school, when the Tribal Leader's son came up and punched me in the face. I made the mistake of defending myself and fighting back, and actually "won" that fight. No sooner had my attacker scurried back across the courtyard than an entire pack of seventh and eighth graders gang-tackled me and did enough physical and emotional damage to send me home for the day. Every day after that, I was kicked, punched, spit on, or pinched, solely due to the color of my skin. Lying in the dirt and grease under a pickup truck was serenity compared to the cruel reality outside the school building. That garage became my refuge from racism.

Eventually the school found out and disallowed me from using the hiding place. I decided to purposefully fail my math class so I would be "forced" to stay inside with a tutor during recess, instead of playing outside with the other kids. I was happy with my decision to become one of the dull bulbs who needed extra time and attention from teachers because it sheltered me from the abuse and discrimination.

I was fortunate the reservation didn't have a tribal high school. Graduating students were funneled into a much larger public high school about 20 miles off the reservation, and I was suddenly in the majority ethnic population (Caucasian); I was no longer being discriminated against. My Native American Indian classmates, who had once been in the majority, were now minority students getting picked on by their Caucasian classmates. Shockingly, about 40 percent of Native American freshmen dropped out within the first two weeks. Essentially, the reservation system, which had been a protective bubble, now worked against the Indian kids in that they had been ill-prepared for the reality of a very different demographic world.

Interestingly, in my new demographic world, I found that even though I was no longer the object of discrimination, it was impossible to shake off the knowledge of what it was like to be harassed and terrorized because you are different. I may not have realized it at the time, but my childhood experience with diversity shaped my outlook on life, and subsequently, my career path.

The indelible impression left on my psyche led me down the path of developing surveys that help improve relationships between people and cultivate a common good. When I founded HR Solutions in 1995, the core concept was, and still is, to help organizations treat their people better by surveying employees and customers, and allowing them to voice what they love about the organization and what could be improved.

A major focus has always been promoting diversity efforts in the workplace. Through our survey and consulting research, we have found a strong correlation between Diversity Satisfaction, Overall Job Satisfaction, and Employee Engagement. For businesses, this means employees who are satisfied with the diversity at their organization are much more likely to feel positively about being a part of the company. This equates to increased discretionary effort and return on investment from employees, the bottom-line benefits of Employee Engagement. To attract and engage top talent, it is essential for organizations to not only employ a diverse staff, but make a continuous effort to ensure all employees and customers are treated with the same respect.

In summary, I have made it my personal mission to educate others on the astounding and wonderful differences in people of various ethnicities, ages, religions, and genders. Fostering a diverse culture is not only the right thing to do, but it leads to better business outcomes. I truly believe teaching the value of diversity to adults will trickle down to their children and create a different reality for future generations. I am sure all parents want their children to live in a world where they can play with their friends during recess, instead of hiding from other students.

Physical Disabilities

People with physical disabilities are a part of a diverse workplace culture, yet they are often overlooked. For example, it is extremely rare to see a person who is wheelchair-bound portrayed as a highly successful business person. This mirrors society's view of people with disabilities—they often are forgotten or not seen as an important part of the workplace. The Americans with Disabilities Act (ADA) was passed in 1990 to guarantee civil rights to those with physical disabilities. In terms of obtaining equal rights, this minority group is fairly new to inclusion. Although more than 20 years have gone by since this act was passed, many organizations have not made a great deal of progress in incorporating individuals with physical disabilities into the workplace. According to recent research, companies are missing an opportunity to obtain high-caliber talent as well as engage nondisabled employees.

A study from the Job Accommodation Network (JAN)[5] has found powerful evidence that employing people who are physically disabled is not only good for overall Employee Engagement, but often costs less in the long run than employing a non-disabled person. Fifty-six percent of the organizations that have made accommodations for an employee with disabilities said the accommodations cost absolutely nothing. Another 37 percent experienced a one-time cost, which averaged $600. The majority of these organizations have experienced a significant return on investment of both their time and money. Employees with disabilities have tenure of about seven years, which is much higher than the average tenure for employees who are not disabled. According to JAN, it can be much more challenging for a person with disabilities to find a job that is a good fit, so he tends to be much more loyal to his employer than employees without disabilities.

In addition, 62 percent of organizations reported that accommodating employees with disabilities improved company morale overall, and 59 percent reported an increase in company productivity. To further drive home the point, 32 percent reported increased profitability, and 18 percent experienced an increase in customer base.

Increasing Minority Representation

Increasing minority representation can be a complex task, since the goal in hiring is not specifically to hire a candidate of a certain ethnicity or demographic, but to hire the best possible candidate. The key to supporting minority representation is to level the playing field among all candidates. There are several tactical approaches organizations can take to increase diversity.

Widen the Candidate Pool

When there are more candidates to choose from, it is likely there will be a higher number of diverse candidates. Increasing hiring options will help organizations widen the pool of candidates. In addition to posting open positions on job boards, another great option is to work with local and professional organizations for diverse candidate referrals.

If your organization works with a search firm, require a diverse slate of candidates for open positions. Many organizations do not specifically ask for diverse candidates, which can contribute to a lack of diversity in the talent pool presented to them. There is higher competition for diverse candidates in executive-level positions, so succession planning is essential for having diverse hiring options.

Promote Minority Career Advancement

It is not enough to simply employ a diverse population. Organizations must also promote diverse employees to high-level positions. The best way to develop a pipeline of diverse candidates at advanced career levels is to employ diverse employees at lower-level positions and provide a clear path for career advancement within the organization.

For many employees, executive-level positions seem unreachable, just beyond the glass ceiling. For example, if there aren't any openly gay Senior Leaders within the organization, an openly gay employee could assume chances for advancement are slim. This perception can be detrimental for minority Engagement and retention, as Career Development is Key Driver 2 of Engagement. To encourage talented minority employees to stay with a company and thrive, organizations can't just *talk the talk* of minority career advancement, they must *walk the walk*. If C-Suite and Upper Level Management aren't diverse *today*, many employees will assume that diversity won't increase in the foreseeable future, and they could easily resign because of it. Ensure your organization is sending the right message about minority career advancement by *showing* it is possible.

Hold All Accountable for Promoting Diversity

If no one is held accountable for following through on organizational initiatives, much less will be accomplished. The same holds true for diversity. Accountability should not be unloaded onto the HR department; employees and managers also hold responsibilities that play a part in organizational diversity goals.

Efforts for promoting diversity should be assessed through various metrics based on the role of particular positions. Diversity requirements can be built into performance expectations and assessed at review time.

Internal diversity audits are a best practice. Senior management and diversity leaders should have a clear understanding of the demographic breakout and reasoning behind past hiring, promotion, and termination decisions. Such an audit can reveal the success level of various action plans, as well as areas for improvement in the future.

Recognize Excellence

Employees should be aware of diversity efforts and successes at the organizational and individual level. This is a critical part of showing commitment to diversity and affecting Engagement. There are many options for communicating diversity efforts, including:

- Post a statement of commitment to embracing and promoting diversity in prominent places, ideally in the actual facilities *and* virtually, on the company website or intranet system. This statement should explain why the organization values diversity and how employees benefit from a diverse environment.
- Provide staff with regular updates on organizational diversity news to keep everyone abreast. Updates can include news from Employee Resource Groups , charitable donations made to support diversity, and workplace demographics when minority representation has increased.
- Consider implementing a diversity awards program to recognize individuals who demonstrate a commitment to diversity and inclusion. Showing appreciation to employees who are actively making a difference will encourage more staff members to get involved in diversity initiatives. In addition, it will promote the organization's commitment to improvement.

Encouraging Future Generations

Outreach to minority youth is a great way to establish a diverse pipeline of future candidates. When organizations reach out to children and show them what is possible in the company and its industry, their career path can be impacted. Minority employees could connect with children through speaking at local schools or community centers. Kids could also be invited to tour the organization for a more in-depth view of career options. When more minorities enter an industry, representation naturally increases.

Hoping to increase diversity is not enough. Real change requires the same level of planning put forth to achieve other organizational goals. Creating a documented action plan for increasing minority representation is essential. Goals should be measurable by outcomes to ensure progress can be tracked.

The importance of senior leadership placing a value on diversity efforts is central to making progress. When senior leaders actively show their support for diversity and inclusion, they will be the change agents.

Case Study: Africa.com

Africa.com was launched in February 2010 as a site for people from across the globe to interact with Africa. Its mission statement is clear: *"to change the way the world sees Africa and to be the online portal for the world's engagement with Africa."* The site draws in visitors from all corners of the Earth, including people from Africa, Asia, Australia, and North and South America. Its market is not only racially diverse, but also geographically, socioeconomically, and technologically diverse. As a result, its definition of diversity is expansive.

"In our environment, it's important for us to have diversity because it's relevant to our business," said Teresa Clarke, founder and CEO of Africa.com. *"Being diverse gives us better commercial performance."*[6] In order for diversity to be sustainable, Clarke believes it must have a direct connection to the bottom line. Africa.com's visitors have a number of different needs, from Africans, who are looking for local news and cultural events, to Americans and Europeans, who are interested in going on

a safari. Some may be accessing the site via a dial-up connection, while others are using the fastest broadband in the world. Africa.com also serves the LGBT (lesbian, gay, bisexual, transgender) community, as Cape Town has become one of the world's top international gay tourist destinations thanks to South Africa's 2006 decision to legalize same-sex marriage. Therefore, understanding how their diverse customer base relates to their products and services has a direct impact on their bottom line. Africa.com is constantly working to make sure they are connecting with all of their users.

In order to reach their users, Clarke wanted to build a diverse team. They employ North, South, East, and West Africans, as well as Americans. Africa.com's employees are not only racially and culturally diverse, but also are diverse based on age, gender, and background. Rather than just hiring from the technology sector, Africa.com looked for a group of people with a variety of skills, including former bankers and financial consultants. *"As we consider different issues, it's quite interesting to see how everyone approaches each topic based on their unique skill sets,"* said Clarke (in the interview cited previously). *"Our diversity lends to more creativity to everything we do, and allows us to challenge traditional ways of thinking."* This approach has helped to create a Magnetic Culture where employees look forward to coming to work and are excited about what they are working to create. They are truly drawn to the organization's shared values and culture. Africa.com has also fostered a culture of high performance, which is fairly unusual for an organization of their size. As Clarke said, *"We punch above our weight."*

It is important to remember diversity not only when hiring staff, but also when choosing outside vendors. When creating Africa.com's logo, the company initially considered designers based in the United States. However, all of the proposed designs showed a stereotypical view of Africa based on a common American viewpoint. *"It was all animals, kente cloth, and the shape of Africa!"* recounted Clarke. Instead of continuing its search for American designers, it decided to look outside of the United States, and found a site from Argentina called Guerra Creativa, or the Creative War. Africa.com put up a contest to create its logo on the site, and designers from across South America submitted designs. What Clarke received was quite a bit different from the designs they saw from designers in the United States, as South Americans don't have the same stereotypes of Africa.

Surprisingly, the winning design it picked actually included one of its stereotypes, without its even realizing it. See Figure 6.2. Clarke originally thought the design was an abstract shape, which she liked because if its originality. However, the designer called his logo "The Face of Africa," which Africa .com realized referred to the face of a lion. He said the use of positive and negative space represents what Africa was, what Africa is, and what Africa will be. Considering this new information, Clarke thought the design definitely fit its organization because it showed how a stereotypical image is evolving to encompass something far greater. By considering designs from a diverse pool of candidates, Africa.com was able to find a logo that matched perfectly with its mission statement: *"to change the way the world sees Africa."*

Figure 6.2 Africa.com Winning Design and Current Logo

Employee Resource Groups

An excellent way for organizations to support diversity is through Employee Resource Groups (ERGs). These groups are established and facilitated by employees as a means for offering support for people who have a common interest. Groups are often geared toward a minority demographic that could benefit from having a network of individuals with like backgrounds and common interests. Not only do ERGs increase Employee Engagement by promoting a diverse culture, they also help organizations improve product and service offerings to diverse customers.

Case Study: PepsiCo

PepsiCo, owner of the world's second largest portfolio of billion-dollar food and beverage brands, understands how ERGs can become strategic business partners that assist with tapping into various consumer markets. Employees in ERGs are able to brainstorm ways in which their organization could better reach consumers of a similar background.

"*Our employees have the ability to make a difference and contribute to the company's performance,*" said Cynthia Trudell, Executive Vice President, Human Resources and Chief Personnel Officer of PepsiCo.[7] PepsiCo believes supporting Diversity and Inclusion enables employees to bring their "whole selves" to work, which leads to higher Engagement levels, creativity, and productivity. When employees understand that their diverse background is valued, they feel empowered to share their points of view and suggestions for improving the organization.

PepsiCo's Asian ERG suggested to senior leaders that the organization could increase marketing efforts geared toward Asian traditions and celebrations, specifically those tied to the Indian culture. With the help of the ERG, PepsiCo's marketing team designed products and developed promotions to coincide with a special Indian celebration. The results were very positive, and PepsiCo would not have necessarily seen the opportunity for the campaign without the help of the Asian ERG.

Another success of PepsiCo's ERGs is the development of kosher-certified Gatorade Thirst Quencher® and G2®. The suggestion for kosher products came from two employees, and the organization supported the idea and helped turn it into reality. The employees worked with managers to develop the plan for producing the products and gaining certification, using one of the employee's knowledge of kosher requirements. They also helped create a detailed promotional plan for marketing kosher products to consumers. This initiative has been successful on many fronts:

- It has demonstrated to employees that their ideas are valued.
- It has shown employees and consumers that PepsiCo values diverse people.
- It has increased revenue from offering a unique product.

Trudell says managers at PepsiCo actively encourage employees to join ERGs and reap the benefits they offer, even if meetings or responsibilities occur on company time. *"These groups are pointless if management says you don't have time to participate in them,"* says Trudell. PepsiCo strives to be sensitive to employees' personal sides, and supporting their involvement in ERGs is a simple way to support their staff.

Generational Differences

People are a product of the culture in which they grew up. Culture changes dramatically over the years, producing generations of people with viewpoints specific to the place and time where they came of age. These viewpoints are ingrained into our personalities so deeply that it is unnatural to expect people to change with the times. Although older generations adopt new technology, the essence of who they are will generally remain rooted in the characteristics specific to their generation.

Generational variances are a major factor in workplace diversity. People of different generations can have a hard time understanding and relating to one another, simply due to different cultural norms and expectations. For example, a Millennial is as likely to know what a Davenport is as a Traditionalist is to know about Nintendo DS. (Both were considered hot commodities of their day, especially for entertaining company.) Lack of familiarity with certain terms or ideas can lead to miscommunication. What may be completely normal to one generation can seem rude, ignorant, or unproductive to another. Organizations must address how such viewpoints play a part in workplace communication, and teach employees to better relate to one another.

There are four generations in today's workforce: Traditionalists, Baby Boomers, Generation X, and Millennials. See Figure 6.3. All of these generations have differences and similarities. As an employer, it is your job to understand these dispositions to better engage your team.

Traditionalists: Born 1929–1946

Size: 27 million, 6 million currently employed.

This generation experienced hard financial times in their young lives, followed by more prosperous times later in life. They have a strong sense of duty and sacrifice, a respect for authority, and trust in the government. They value accountability and work ethic, and believe promotions

Figure 6.3 Workforce by Generation

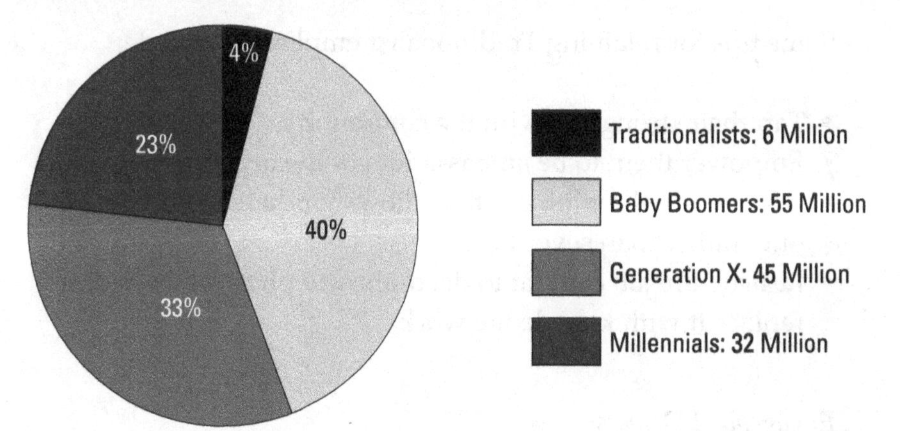

and recognition come with job tenure. Traditionalists are loyal to their employer and expect their employer to be loyal to them in return. They do not hold the belief that work is meant to be fun, and they seek personal fulfillment through other outlets.

Defining Moments

- The Great Depression
- World War II
- The G.I. Bill

Influential People

- Henry Ford
- Charles Lindbergh
- Winston Churchill
- Franklin D. Roosevelt

Retention Tips

Some tips for retaining Traditionalist employees include:

- Tap their strong ties with the community.
- Empower them to be ambassadors of the organization.
- Offer gradual retirement that allows workers to "phase out" rather than sever ties.
- Restructure job content to deemphasize physical work and replace it with knowledge work.

Engagement Drivers

Relevant Engagement Drivers for Traditionalist employees include:

- Key Driver 6: Senior Management's Relationship with Employees
- Key Driver 4: Strategy and Mission—Especially the Freedom and Autonomy to Succeed and Contribute to the Organization's Success

Baby Boomers: Born 1947–1965

Size: 76 million, 55 million currently employed.

This generation was promised "the American Dream" as children, and they work to pursue it. The Civil Rights Movement, the Vietnam War, and the free spirit mentality of the 1960s and 1970s shaped their perspective. Baby Boomers believe in equal rights and opportunities, and are driven by goals for financial success. Throughout most of their lives, times were increasingly more prosperous, which led to consumerism and a "spend now, worry later" mentality. Baby Boomers believe in teamwork and building relationships with others. Their careers oftentimes create their identity, and many "live to work." A work/life imbalance is commonly accepted for this generation.

Defining Moments

- The Civil Rights Movement
- The Cold War
- The assassinations of President John F. Kennedy, Martin Luther King Jr., and Robert Kennedy
- The Vietnam War
- Man walks on the Moon
- The Woodstock festival

Influential People

- The Beatles
- Lee Iacocca
- Henry Kissinger
- Jack Welch

Retention Tips

Retention tips for Baby Boomers include:

- Take a democratic approach within the team.
- Leverage their ability to mentor new employees.
- Offer a flexible environment that balances work and retirement.
- Provide training opportunities to help them stay competitive in the workplace.

Engagement Drivers

Engagement Drivers for Baby Boomers include:

- Key Driver 2: Career Development
- Key Driver 5: Job Content—The Ability to Do What I Do Best

Generation X: Born 1966–1979

Size: 60 million, 45 million currently employed.

Gen X-ers grew up with a great deal of free time. This created a self-reliant generation that values control of their personal time. They are skeptical of authority and do not feel a sense of loyalty is due to their employer. They are more cynical than generations before and after them. They focus on career advancement and skill development, and outcome over process. They question the reasoning behind policies and procedures, and want open communication.

Defining Moments

- The Feminist Movement
- *Schoolhouse Rock*
- The Space Shuttle *Challenger* explodes on takeoff
- The Berlin Wall comes down
- The AIDS epidemic
- The rising divorce rate

Influential People

- Bill Gates
- Steve Jobs
- Michael Jackson
- Madonna
- "The Brat Pack"

Retention Tips

Retention Tips for Gen X-ers include:

- Link their contributions to the "big picture."
- Offer learning and training opportunities.
- Promote employee involvement.
- Be flexible about meeting deadlines.
- Focus on results.

Engagement Drivers

Engagement Drivers for Gen X-ers are:

- Key Driver 4: Strategy and Mission—Especially the Freedom and Autonomy to Succeed and Contribute to the Organization's Success
- Key Driver 7: Open and Effective Communication

Millennials: Born 1980–1992

Size: 88 million, 32 million currently employed.

Millennials grew up being sheltered by their parents and constantly kept busy as children. They work best in a structured environment, where mentors help them improve their skills. Millennials are highly confident and thrive on recognition and instant gratification. They are constant communicators and actively seek direction. In a gargantuan difference between Baby Boomers and Millennials, the latter see their career as one element within their life, not the single element that makes their life. Millennials want their job to provide personal fulfillment and support a positive work/life balance. They are passionate about causes and want to make the world a better place. They have seen from their parents and grandparents that loyalty to an organization does not always lead to stability or success. For this reason, organizations must earn Millennials' trust and loyalty.

Defining Moments

- The Internet
- The 9/11 attacks
- The Columbine massacre

- The War on Terror
- The rise of social networks

Influential People
- Steve Jobs
- Mark Zuckerberg
- Britney Spears
- Venus and Serena Williams
- Prince William and Princess Kate Middleton

Retention Tips

Retention Tips for Millennials include:

- Create a collaborative and feedback-oriented work environment.
- Provide frequent communication.
- Ensure training program is comprehensive.
- Set up a structured, supportive work environment.
- Offer frequent recognition for achievements.
- Provide developmental opportunities.
- Suggest volunteer opportunities.
- Link with on-call mentors.
- Use cross-training techniques.

Engagement Drivers

Engagement Drivers for Millennials include:

- Key Driver 1: Recognition
- Key Driver 10: Organizational Culture and Core/Shared Values
- Key Driver 8: Coworker Satisfaction/Cooperation—The Unsung Hero of Retention

Generational diversity can easily be an organizational strength, or the root cause for internal tension. It is vital to recognize the differences and similarities of the various generations in the workforce to foster an environment that supports all employees.

Millennials: You Don't "Retain" Them, You "Evolve" Them

Millennials have made up at least one-quarter of the workforce since 2009.[8] This number is on the rise as mature generations continue to retire. Since Millennials are the fastest growing generation in the workplace, and other generations have had the least amount of time to get accustomed to what makes Millennials tick, I want to focus on this demographic.

First and foremost, historically, the youngest generation entering the workforce has always caused a stir with older workers. When you entered the workforce—whether you are a Gen X-er, Baby Boomer, or Traditionalist—people of other generations wondered what your generation was thinking too. Social norms naturally change over time, and the youngest generation is always driving and aligning with the changes. The variance in viewpoints and outlook often makes it challenging for different generations to relate to one another. However, by simply gaining an understanding of what factors cause different generations to think and behave as they do, managers will be better able to engage their employees and foster an environment that supports *all* generations.

Communication Norms

Millennials' perceptions of the working world reflect modern culture. Technology has molded Millennials into being a generation that communicates frequently. While some Millennials might have had pen pals in elementary school, most could not imagine a delay of a week or more for someone to receive a message. It is very common for Millennials to text message their friends back and forth all day long, every day. With several hundred "friends" just a tweet or status update away, Millennials enjoy keeping each other in the loop about what is going on in their daily lives.

The ease of social interaction has shaped Millennials' views on communication norms to be much different than older generations. Even voice mail can seem outdated to Millennials, who often prefer to read their communication and keep a permanent record of it for future reference. The preference for constant virtual communication is totally normal to Millennials, which carries over into the workplace. Older generations oftentimes have difficulty relating to this need, and feel out of their element when communicating virtually. On the flip side, a professional tone in writing does not always come easily for Millennials, who are used to communicating in 140 characters or fewer. When pressured to communicate through methods they are less familiar with, delivering a clear message and understanding the nuances of etiquette can be more difficult for employees. Training sessions can be extremely beneficial to help employees understand the generational differences in communication norms.

Courtney Pike, Vice President of Job Bound Outplacement and JB Training Solutions, specializes in workplace training and coaching on generational differences. Her firm's expertise lies in teaching Millennials how to transition from college to the working world, as well as helping managers relate to this unique generation. Pike manages a team of Millennial employees, and prides herself for creating a workplace environment that is Millennial-friendly.

She was meeting with her team once a day to stay abreast of their projects and provide them with designated time to ask questions. Although she felt meeting on a daily basis was more often than necessary, she wanted to cater to Millennials' need for direction and guidance. After several weeks, her team came to her and said they wanted to talk to her about the frequency of their meetings. *"Meeting with you once a day has been really great,"* one young team member said. *"But we've been talking and think we should change how often we meet."* Pike was thrilled the team finally felt confident enough that they no longer wanted to meet every day. *"Of course we can adjust it!"* she said. *"Great!"* the Millennials replied. *"We would like to meet twice a day. We just aren't receiving enough direction when we only meet once a day."*[9] Brad Karsh, President of Job Bound Outplacement and JB Training Solutions, loves to tell this story because it is the perfect example of how Millennials are different from other generations.

In addition to better communication technology, Millennials grew up with more activities where they were given direction by a coach, instructor, or tutor.

"They are used to looking up and having someone tell *them what to do,"* says Karsh. Since Millennials are used to structure and direction, they feel most comfortable in an environment where they know exactly what they are supposed to do and precisely how to do it. This attitude is different from generations before them. *"The greatest gift you can give to Gen X-ers and Baby Boomers is to assign them a project, give them two weeks to do it, and tell them to figure it out,"* says Karsh. *"If you do that to Millennials, they freak out. They are back in their manager's office 10 minutes later with 17 questions."*[10]

This variance in preference for direction is a common area where different generations bump heads. Older managers think they are providing their direct reports with excellent direction, but younger employees often disagree. They can feel as though their manager is purposefully providing limited information and do not understand why. Perceived lack of proper communication can be a powerful demagnetizer, so managers must adapt their communication style to be effective with Millennials.

A Special Generation

Millennials are often thought of by other generations as the self-important demographic in the workforce. Millennials' attitudes stem from how they have been raised as children, in a culture where *everyone* is special. Older generations have actively avoided hurting the self-esteem of Millennial children, by praising and recognizing them much more often than they were recognized as children. In essence, first place, second place, and third place ribbons are now accompanied by fourth place, fifth place, and sixth place ribbons, and beyond.

Through his workshops with Millennials, Karsh has found that they like to be recognized an average of seven times per day. This certainly was not the norm for past generations. As a personal best practice giving frequent Recognition, I try to always respond to my Millennial employees' e-mails the same day, even just to say "thanks." This lets employees know I received what they sent me, read it, and appreciate their effort.

In some ways, the cultural shift in Recognition has empowered Millennials by boosting their confidence and instilling a belief that they can accomplish anything they set out to do. In other ways, it has made them expectant of Recognition and attention to a degree that can be challenging in the working environment. According to many studies, young people have become much more self-centered and narcissistic than in years past. In fact, according to the Narcissistic Personality Inventory (NPI), there was a 30 percent increase in the average level of narcissism in college students from 1982 to 2006.[11] This 40-item Personal Assessment is a widespread psychological index used to assess personality traits, including entitlement, superiority, self-sufficiency, and vanity. It includes items such as, *"If I ruled the world, it would be a better place,"* and *"I think I am a special person."* While there are no "right" or "wrong" answers, the total number of responses deemed to coincide with narcissism show a general level of the perception of one's place in society.

Some items in the Personal Assessment are a direct reflection of life experience, such as, *"I know that I am good because everyone keeps telling me so."* Responses to this item show how self-image can be influenced by how people are treated. The trending in increased overall scores of college students since the 1980s likely reflects a shift in how society has treated children. In essence, Millennials have been raised to believe they are unique individuals who can accomplish anything. This disposition is not good or bad, it's just different from other generations.

Giving Back

It is important to note that empowering Millennials has resulted in many supremely positive outcomes. Overall, Millennials have a very high value for volunteerism and service, a trait often associated with Traditionalists. The Millennials' can-do attitude is the basis for shaping a new cultural outlook on helping others. Millennials are making a positive impact on corporate social responsibility (CSR) trends simply by considering employers' efforts when determining the full value of working for an organization. In fact, CSR is the third most impactful Engagement Driver of Millennials, and organizations are adjusting their Engagement approach to meet, and even exceed, Millennials' expectations.

Millennials are also taking more of an interest in improving the environment than any generation before them, an initiative that will have exponential results in years to come. In addition, the ultimate test of service values has been shown through Millennials taking the initiative to serve their country in the War on Terror, some doing multiple tours.

Millennials are certainly different than past generations, and organizations have countless ways to benefit from the traits and skills they have to offer. To support Engagement and build a culture that is magnetic to all generations, it is imperative to embrace generational differences.

Profitability

Employee diversity greatly impacts profitability in numerous ways. First and foremost in building a Magnetic Culture, diversity has a positive correlation to Employee Engagement. As employees become more satisfied with diversity at their organization, Engagement levels will increase. We've already proven how increasing Engagement impacts your bottom line, so the same results apply to improving diversity.

A diverse staff will also be more successful in serving diverse customers, whether locally or internationally. When employees can relate to their organization's target market, they will have a better understanding of customers' needs, which enables better customer service. A positive customer experience is the best public relations you can get, so catering to your diverse customer base and building relationships with them should be a priority.

Diversity promotes innovation. When people bring unique experiences to the table, employees can learn from one another to develop new ideas for products or services that cater to diverse people. Employees' personal experiences can be beneficial for providing insight in creating new offerings that drive market share. Seizing the opportunity to capitalize on the benefits of diversity will take you into a new and better realm of doing business.

Recognize and Celebrate

Our differences should not be ignored; they should be recognized and celebrated. The bottom line is that organizations and managers who are not valuing, appreciating, and managing diversity are never going to achieve the same level of greatness in business outcomes as those who are. Diversity affects everyone. At your organization, it can either be a competitive business advantage, or a roadblock to success.

Chapter 7

ENGAGEMENT TRENDS

The best way to predict the future is to create it.

—Peter Drucker

Following changing Engagement trends will benefit the employer-employee relationship and your organization as a whole. Whether introducing a more casual environment or addressing issues through open communication, the workplace, and how employees react to its environment, is evolving. To embrace these trends, is to engage your employees.

A job should *not* be all work and no play. This important aspect of the work environment has been left out of the equation for far too long, but some smart employers have recently realized the impact a little fun can have on Employee Engagement, and they are not turning back.

Fun Linked to Engagement

Recently, many companies have begun providing unique levity-building benefits to create a Magnetic Culture that attracts and retains an organization's best talent. Engaged

Employees are 3.5 times more likely to stay with their employer, lowering turnover costs.[1] Creating an environment where employees are having fun while performing great work makes good business sense.[2]

Case Study: Radio Flyer—Success Should Be Fun

It is bright, shiny, new, and it can take you places you never dreamed possible. Although I could be alluding to a certain little red wagon, I am actually referring to a career with Radio Flyer. Many people around the world know that Radio Flyer has been making children happy for generations, but people may not know the same holds true for its employees. With more than 10 awards in the past few years for being a top employer, including HR Solutions' Best-in-Class Award, the organization is attracting attention by simply understanding that adults want to have fun too.

On their first day at Radio Flyer, new hires receive a welcome wagon that goes far beyond a typical meet and greet; they receive an actual Radio Flyer wagon to take home and "play" with so they can reconnect with the fun-loving child within. Senior Leadership understands feeling valued and appreciated is a Key Driver of Employee Engagement, so making employees (aka "Flyers") feel immediately welcome is essential. Receiving a literal welcome wagon also connects Flyers (and their families!) to the brand, which fosters strong employee and family support from day one.

The fun does not stop for Flyers after the first day on the job. Creating a fun and rewarding culture for staff members at all seniority levels is a top priority. Flyers are shown that their hard work is recognized through various events and awards. Radio Flyer parties and celebrations are held regularly to encourage camaraderie. Celebrations occur about once a month and range from the December holiday party, where all Flyers receive their choice of a honey baked ham or a fruit basket, to "Maya del Sol," the surprise celebration where Flyers find out they can leave work early to enjoy food, drinks, and a mariachi band. The Halloween party is a Flyer favorite, as it is one of the biggest celebrations of the year. Flyers look forward to participating in a highly competitive pumpkin-carving contest and costume contest. Robert Pasin, Chief Wagon Officer (CWO) of Radio Flyer, believes providing activities that serve as a creative outlet is beneficial to a Flyer's well-being and helps shape a fun company culture.

Fun even finds its way into company businesses cards, which show a composite of a cartoon body on a wagon with a photo of the Flyer's head to personalize each card. See Figure 7.1.

In addition to company events, Radio Flyer has several different awards programs to formally recognize individuals for their hard work. At the "Breakfast of Customer Service Champions," Senior Leadership serves breakfast to staff members and honors top performers in various departments.

Figure 7.1 Radio Flyer Business Card

In addition, on-site massages are offered during "Customer Service Week" to thank staff for their efforts in providing "fast, friendly, and effective service." Flyers are also acknowledged at monthly company meetings and asked to present information about key successes. These opportunities to be recognized in front of their peers are valued highly by staff members. Pasin believes it is also important for the Executive-level staff to get personally involved in showing Recognition. As a best practice, he writes a personalized thank-you note to every Flyer on their yearly anniversary with the company.

Radio Flyer has long fostered a company culture that promotes staff member feedback; managers thought they would receive more candid responses if Flyers were given a chance to respond anonymously. Senior Leadership also wanted to measure Flyer Engagement to take a pulse of how successful their efforts had been, and learn areas for improvement in policy and culture.

In 2009, Radio Flyer partnered with HR Solutions to conduct an Employee Engagement Survey and subsequent action planning. The survey results showed that Radio Flyer was far above international Employee Engagement norms in every single dimension for both their U.S. and China locations. The overwhelming theme of staff feedback showed that 80 to 90 percent of Flyers responded favorably to each item included in the survey. For some items, these results were more than 40 percentage points above normative scores.

The most favorable responses from the U.S. office included:

"This organization makes it possible for employees to directly contribute to its success."

- Radio Flyer: 98 percent agree
- Normative score: 69 percent

"I am satisfied with the various events this organization uses to show its appreciation of employees (such as Holiday party, service awards, employee of the month, etc.)."

- Radio Flyer: 98 percent agree
- Normative score: 67 percent agree

"My supervisor lets employees know when they have done a good job."

- Radio Flyer: 94 percent agree
- Normative score: 70 percent agree

"Senior management of this organization is concerned about the employees."

- Radio Flyer: 94 percent agree
- Normative score: 54 percent agree

These results earned Radio Flyer Best-in-Class scores, showing the organization was competitive even within the top 10 percent of all organizations surveyed. Radio Flyer's lowest scoring survey items were still 7 percentage points higher than the norm, and by many standards, worthy of celebration.

Even though these survey scores were well above average, Radio Flyer still made an effort to improve. As a direct result of great management and direction, Radio Flyer's most recent Employee Engagement Survey results showed 92 percent of Flyers look forward to coming to work every day. (And it is not just because of regular company tricycle races!) Radio Flyer's best practices in creating an environment that attracts and retains top talent serve as an example for organizations across all industries.[3]

Even if your organization doesn't specialize in making toys, there are still plenty of opportunities to incorporate elements of fun that will shape the culture and act like a magnet for top talent. A great way to draw people to the organization is through the brand itself. By creating positive experiences for customers, organizations will manage and shape their brand. When an organization is known for its fun and lighthearted attitude, Engaged employees will be attracted to become part of such an environment.

Case Study: Groupon

Splashing into the scene in 2008 by offering daily deals online and catering to local markets, Groupon™ has transformed the way people shop. With international Groupon mania and a quickly growing customer base who know the organization for its fun, carefree image, Groupon has high expectations to live up to when it comes to employment.

However, as Dan Jessup, Head of People Strategy at Groupon, put it, *"You can't just throw a pool table in your office and expect the culture to change."*[4] Jessup should know. The corporate culture of Groupon seeps into everything they do, from the quirky writing style on its website to their job descriptions and company celebrations. Groupon even has a unique e-mail unsubscribe page where the *Punish Derrick* video shows "the guy who thought you would enjoy receiving the daily Groupon e-mails." The person unsubscribing sees a video with Derrick being punished for adding him or her to the e-mail list. *"You don't do one singular thing that makes a company fun or cool,"* said Jessup. *"It's having consistent behavior and attitudes. That stuff creates something that has permanence."*

Jessup has found that the power of humor within their offices is twofold.

- First, of course, is that it provides great comic relief on the job.

- Second, and more importantly, it provides context for what they do every day.

Through humor, employees of Groupon are able to step back from their work to see the big picture and keep themselves grounded. At the Chicago headquarters of Groupon, the use of humor has helped to build a lively atmosphere where employees take their jobs seriously, but don't take themselves too seriously.

Humor has been a part of Groupon since its beginning. One of the reasons it has become such an integral component of their culture is because it comes down from the very top, Groupon's CEO, Andrew Mason. When Mason founded Groupon, he did so with a firm belief that the company should never be boring. This idea helped the organization develop a rich personality all of its own.

Besides humor, the personality of Groupon also includes a strong sense of inclusion and ownership among employees. Employees truly feel like they *are* Groupon. This sense of inclusion is aided by the use of the plural first-person, "we," in company communication, instead of "you." "We" helps employees see that they are part of a whole, and an integral component of Groupon.

A sense of inclusion is also built in to the decision-making process at Groupon. While all of its employees cannot participate in every decision, they still feel included and informed, thanks to strong internal communication. The company's goal is to help employees understand exactly why and how decisions are made. In addition, employees are strongly encouraged to alert management of any processes or policies that are roadblocks to their productivity. Mason created an e-mail address with the user name "Kill Bureaucracy" for employees to directly send any concerns about overly engineered processes. This direct pipeline to the top encourages

Groupon to constantly change and adapt to the business climate, as well as build its inclusive corporate culture.

Ultimately, the unique personality of Groupon has helped it organically build a Magnetic Culture where employees want to work hard and stay with the company, which is the true benefit of their corporate culture. As Jessup said, *"You can have all the badass employees you want, but if they don't feel engaged in what they do, then they aren't going to stick around."*

Companies do not need to be household names or have industry-leading profits to create a Magnetic Culture. Studies have shown implementing small and inexpensive changes can drastically affect Employee Engagement. Try implementing some of the following changes to help create a fun workplace environment:

1. Cater breakfast or lunch once a month and encourage employees to take a break and socialize with colleagues.
2. Have a "Traveling Trophy" to recognize a person or department that has done an excellent job. If an organization has multiple locations, the trophy can be awarded to different locations each month and mailed back and forth.
3. Schedule a group volunteer activity where employees can work together for a good cause. This can easily be done in the office by making crafts or cards for the elderly or children at a local hospital.
4. Raffle off sports tickets or small gift cards to employees and donate the raffle profits to the winner's favorite charity.
5. Engrave bricks to build a "wall or path of fame." The bricks can be engraved with messages acknowledging employee accomplishments that have had a positive impact on the organization.
6. Have a "suitcase party," where one lucky employee wins a free weekend getaway on the company's dime. Employees bring a packed suitcase and depart the same day.

7. Create a suggestion "tackle box" as a means for employees to submit innovative ideas. Reward employees for ideas the organization can use to increase Engagement or lower costs.
8. Schedule a yearly staff appreciation party for employees and their families and friends to attend. Encouraging employees to invite their loved ones illustrates the company's desire to learn more about its employees and their personal lives.
9. Create "Staff Info Cards" that feature a picture of each employee with fun facts and major accomplishments. The cards can be hung in the entrance of your organization to emphasize the importance of people.
10. Start a staff library where employees can check out books. Employees can donate their own books to the library, and the organization can supplement the collection by purchasing books as well.

All of these tips will add fun to the workplace and create a culture where employees feel valued. Taking the time to go above and beyond in creating a great workplace environment pays Talent Management dividends.

Do Employees Have to Dress Professionally to Act Professionally?

Dress code policies walk a fine line between portraying a professional image to clients and customers, while allowing employees to be comfortable and productive. In recent years, more and more organizations are walking that line in tennis shoes.

In our parents' and grandparents' generations, working in an office generally meant dressing up for work every day. It did not matter the industry or if employees ever came in contact with customers or clients. Even uniforms were significantly dressier than today's standards. People dressed up because it was the social norm to do so at the time. In fact, there are a number of events outside of the workplace that were once considered opportunities to dress up: traveling by train or plane, going grocery shopping, and even picking the children up from school. Over the years, people seem to have come to the conclusion that the effort of dressing up could be better spent in other ways.

As dressing casually has become the trend in modern culture, many organizations are following suit. Even multibillion-dollar businesses, such as Microsoft, Facebook, and Netflix, stress the importance of comfort over style in the workplace. While the Microsoft website advises job candidates to wear business attire to their interviews, it has been said by some pundits that jeans and sandals are the daily norm there.

When employees are free to wear what they choose, it can be an attractive benefit of working for the company. Not only do most people find it more convenient and comfortable to wear what they choose, but the absence of dress code rules sends a message to employees that they are respected and trusted to make good decisions on their own. This message helps build the foundation of a Magnetic Culture.

Determining the Right Dress Code

While casual dress codes may work for organizations in modern industries, does a lax dress code look unprofessional in traditionally conservative fields? It depends, but that might be a line better walked in loafers, instead of flipflops. The way in which employees present themselves can make a big difference in how clients and customers view an organization. If employees regularly meet with clients who dress professionally, the organization will likely be more successful if its employees dress professionally as well. The same holds true for organizations that provide professional services to the public. Customers will likely have more trust in the quality of service if employees present a professional image. The challenge is creating a dress code policy that allows employees to be comfortable and look professional at the same time.

If employees are not in front of clients or customers, a company's motives for upholding a dress code are often different. A major reason many organizations have a traditional business or business casual dress code is to promote an internal image of a professional working environment. If employees dress professionally, they will act professionally, right? If only it were that easy.

Although dressing professionally can suggest an employee will be in a business mind-set in the workplace, it by no means should be viewed as a behavior regulator. A person in a suit and tie will not necessarily act any more professionally than a person in jeans and a sweatshirt. (The term *white-collar crime* proves this point to a tee.) If an organization is concerned with upholding a professional work environment, this issue could be better addressed in regards to behavior standards and office etiquette, rather than solely tying professionalism to a business dress code.

When forming a dress code policy, Senior Leadership should focus on the end result of what they are trying to achieve and tailor the policy to specifically meet those goals. Including additional policies just for the sake of having a "more complete" dress code can be viewed negatively by employees and send a message that the company is controlling of its employees. In addition, instead of just communicating the dress code policy to employees, Senior Leadership should provide information on *why* the policy is in place. When employees understand the reasoning behind company policies, they are much more likely to comply.

Ask for Feedback

A great way for Senior Leadership to maintain rapport with employees is to ask for feedback on the organization's dress code policy. If your organization has a large Millennial population, you are likely to find that a casual dress code would be appreciated. If employees feel strongly about making certain changes, doing so could be an easy way to increase Employee Engagement.

Results from our own recent Employee Engagement Survey revealed that employees unanimously wanted to switch from business casual to casual clothing, so they could wear jeans and tennis shoes. Our leadership team discussed changing the dress code, and we decided that since it was so important to our staff, we could make the change. The only exception would be that on days when clients are visiting our office the policy would go back to business casual in order to uphold a professional appearance.

When we announced the new policy in our companywide meeting, people literally screamed and jumped for joy. It was, by far, the most positive response I have ever received from an announcement or policy change. It is ironic that something so simple (and cost-free) can have a more profound response than other initiatives that have taken significantly more time and money. It just goes to show what an impact this particular topic can have on building a Magnetic Culture.

When forming a dress code policy, it is important to keep clients, customers, and employees in mind. Although catering to clients and customers is important, maintaining an engaged and productive staff should also be a top priority.[5]

Recognizing and Addressing Stress

Stress is a reality for employees in all industries. While stress levels obviously vary from person to person, it is one job aspect nearly all employees experience on some level. Rather than turning a blind eye to this issue, a recent workplace trend is addressing it through open communication between employees and employers.

Simply thinking about the upcoming workday can sometimes be enough to fill overworked employees with a sense of impending dread. Worrying about a never-ending to-do list can cause chronic anxiety, even for top performers. In fact, 66 percent of employees believe they currently suffer from job stress.[6] Importantly, I believe the people who experience the most stress generally care the most about the organization and doing a great job: the Engaged employees. To combat job stress, rather than losing top talent to burnout managers must tackle the issue of stress head on with open communication.

Employees must be told that experiencing stress on the job does not mean they are not up to snuff for their position. Many employees can be scared to talk about being overwhelmed with a heavy workload, for fear of being perceived negatively by their manager. No one wants to come across as lazy or as a complainer with a bad attitude. As a manager, it is essential to have open communication with direct reports about how stress is oftentimes simply not only a reality of the working world, but of life in general. As a team, colleagues should want to help reduce one another's stress whenever possible, and employees should be encouraged to speak up when they need help.

Even the best of employees can quickly go from actively engaged to ambivalent to actively disengaged after suffering from ongoing job stress. This drop in Engagement levels can lead to decreased productivity, decreased profitability, increased absenteeism, and ultimately increased turnover.

Stress also can have a detrimentally negative impact on one's physical and mental health. Physically, stress can cause high blood pressure, suppress the immune system, and increase the risk of stroke and heart attack. Stress can also affect one's body weight, as stressed individuals often do not eat right or hit the gym, both due to stress itself and a perceived lack of time for these activities. Psychologically, stress can lead to anxiety and depression.

What Can Organizations Do to Manage Stress?

Managers should *take the initiative* to ensure their employees are not stressed due to an overwhelming workload. There are several best practices that managers and leadership teams can follow to help reduce stress levels in the workplace:

- Conduct "stress check-ins."
- Balance workloads.
- Give employees the reins.
- Create wellness programs.
- Encourage laughter.

Conduct "Stress Check-ins"

Regularly meet with employees to make sure their workloads are manageable. These meetings will help employees feel comfortable talking about stress and seeking help when over-stressed. When possible, attempt to rearrange responsibilities among the team.

Balance Workloads

Managers have a tendency to rely too heavily on their star players because they know these employees will do a great job every time. However, managers often do not realize,that their best employees have been worked to the bone, until it is too late. To avoid burnout, make sure that responsibilities are spread *evenly* throughout the team.

Give Employees the Reins

When employees have a sense of control over their workload, it can help to reduce their stress levels. To increase employee control, allow employees the autonomy to set their own deadlines and manage their own projects, whenever possible.

Create Wellness Programs

Each year, companies spend about 1.5 to 3 percent of payroll on unplanned absences, such as sick days and extended leave. However, according to a study published in the *American Journal of Health Promotion*, health care costs rose at a 15 percent slower rate among wellness program participants than that of a comparison group when employers consistently offered a wellness program.[7]

Exercising can reduce stress levels because it relaxes muscles and triggers the release of endorphins. Unfortunately, stressed individuals tend to avoid going to the gym, so they oftentimes do not reap the stress-reduction benefits of exercise. Offering programs with incentives to participate, such as reduced-cost gym memberships, can help to encourage employees to participate.

Organizations can also offer other wellness-related programs, such as nutritional counseling, weight loss/management clubs, and smoking cessation support. Many employers regularly offer on-site 15-minute massages that employees can take advantage of during the workday. This particular initiative is usually a big hit with employees.

Encourage Laughter

Frankly, we spend far too much time working not to be laughing more often. Five-year-olds laugh an average of 113 times per day. As we get older, this number continues to decrease until it bottoms out in adulthood— from age 44 to retirement with only 11 times per day.[8] Studies have shown that laughter relaxes muscles, lowers blood pressure, and speeds the flow of oxygen through the body, which ultimately reduce stress levels. In addition, both smiling and laughing release endorphins into the brain. Encouraging laughter in the workplace is a great way to make a positive impact on both company culture and employees' wellness.

Responsibility for Stress Management

The responsibility for stress management should not fall entirely on the shoulders of the Management team. Employees need to take the initiative to go to their managers when they are facing a heavy workload that is a little too hard to handle. In addition, employees can take control when they learn to effectively manage their time. Staying organized, creating and following a detailed to-do list every day, and setting appropriate deadlines can all help to reduce stress levels. When employees know how to take control of their stress, thinking about work should not cause worry or anxiety. Instead, employees can once again feel the excitement for work they felt their very first day on the job.[9]

Work/Life Balance

The majority of people spend more hours at work than they do with family or friends. Unfortunately, 90 percent of American mothers and 95 percent of American fathers report work-family conflict.[10] While engaged employees are motivated and dedicated to their organization, it is important for employers to recognize these employees need time away from the workplace to *stay* engaged.

There are countless ways for supporting a positive work/life balance; however, the key is to offer options. Employees have different needs, so allowing choices is the best way to support a diverse staff. Flexibility in scheduling is a major bonus for many employees. This added value oftentimes makes employees appreciate their position more than they would have otherwise, which leads to commitment to the organization and builds a strong foundation for Engagement. Adjustable scheduling can also help attract top talent; 72 percent said flexible work arrangements would cause them to choose one job over another.[11]

To build a Magnetic Culture, it is crucial for employers to take the time to create a means for employees to have a healthy balance between the workplace and their personal lives. This arena is one where organizations can get creative to develop unique offerings that truly set them apart from the competition. A few colorfully inventive options are the following:

1. Rather than classifying the work week as five days long, allow employees to work four 10-hour shifts. This schedule enables employees to have three days off each week instead of the typical two-day weekend.
2. When possible, incorporate a work-from-home policy. Offering this benefit even a few days per year can make a difference.
3. Make day care available to staff on-site or incorporate a benefit which would provide day care at a discounted rate.

4. Establish a deal with a local dry-cleaning service or even consider having one on-site.
5. Offer a tax preparation service benefit.
6. Offer free gift-wrapping services during the holidays and for special occasions.
7. Consider presenting high-performing employees with family vacation packages in addition to, or in place of, monetary bonuses.
8. Offer concierge services to help employees balance the many errands in life.
9. Offer scheduling of flextime, where employees can provide their input on their preferred work schedule (7 a.m. to 4 p.m., 8 a.m. to 5 p.m., 9 a.m. to 6 p.m.). If multiple employees request the same shift, offer a rotating schedule to satisfy everyone.
10. Offer seasonal hours when employees can leave early on Fridays during certain times of the year.
11. Make yearly anniversaries with the company an extra paid time off (PTO) day to encourage employees to celebrate their tenure. This day off will also serve as a reminder that their employer cares.
12. Encourage employees to avoid checking their work e-mail and voice mail after the workday and on weekends, to separate work from their personal lives.
13. Allow employees to take a longer lunch, if they come in early or work later, to make up the missed time. This option will make it easier for staff to schedule appointments or run errands on their break.
14. Hold virtual meetings, so employees do not have to be on-site to attend.
15. Encourage employees to take frequent breaks to rehydrate and go to the restroom (at least once every two hours). This may seem unnecessary to address, but many busy people forget to take time out of the day for their personal well-being.

While you may not be able to initiate all of these suggestions, even tackling a few will help employees see your organization's concern for true work/life balance in the workplace. Address these recommendations with your Leadership Team as soon as possible to tailor your approach and set your plan into action.

Multinational Engagement

Employee Engagement challenges often increase exponentially as an organization's size and locations multiply. The best practices for engaging diverse, multinational teams are similar to those used to engage employees in any organization. However, implementing such practices across continents often requires a shift from granular initiatives to high-level goals that involve thousands of people. A sustained, organized effort that recognizes and embraces cultural differences is the key to supporting multinational Engagement.

Case Study: Engagement—Defining Basic Needs

For one industry-leading health care organization with 90,000 employees worldwide, Engagement strategies are complex and diversified. A culture that attracts and retains employees is inherently different throughout the world. The global nature of this health care company leads to the challenge of understanding the nuances of local culture and catering an employee experience that meets those needs.

An HR Director at this organization references the shift in some parts of the world from concern for "nice-to-have" workplace benefits to essential benefits, such as clean water. Employees in the Indonesian locations have access to clean water when they are at work, but many do not when they go home. This is a major factor that affects employees' well-being, and it is something Senior Leaders need to know in order to make the most meaningful impact.

Improving talent management strategy in this region is not going to be a priority if people do not have the basic needs for themselves and their families at home. Addressing how to improve employees' access to clean water at home has been the focal point for improving Engagement. Ameliorating employees' welfare outside of the workplace truly shows the organization's commitment to the *Human* in Human Capital.

For staff in the Brazilian locations, Engagement starts with safety. Employees in Brazil face considerable danger outside of the workplace, including simply commuting to and from the office safely. Many employees commute long distances to their office, and carjackings and muggings are extremely common. Even leaving the building for a coffee break can put employees at risk for violence. In this unique situation, employee safety came to the forefront of building a Magnetic Culture in that region.

The concern for personal safety throughout the workday comes first, according to HR executives. Referring back to Maslow's Hierarchy of Needs (Figure 3.1), Safety is the second tier, just above Physiological Needs, and below Love/Belonging, Esteem, and Self-Actualization. Managers in Brazil recognize employee safety as being part of the foundation for the employee value proposition (EVP), so they have chosen to make creating a safe working environment a top priority.

To address unique regional challenges, managers in each country are given the power to administer their own local budget. Since these professionals work closely with their local teams, Senior Executives believe they are in the best position to make decisions on what initiatives would have the biggest impact on their unique culture. Through Survey Action Teams, managers in Brazil learned of the need for a place where employees could get food and drinks without leaving the safety of the building. Since managers are empowered to use their budget as they see fit, they were able to expedite the process of building a café in the lobby where employees could gather without facing the danger of the streets. The addition of the café is seen by employees as a significant and meaningful benefit. It has allowed staff members to reduce their stress level while on the job, as well as increase employee camaraderie from spending more time with colleagues.

This organization's Engagement strategies are as unique as their diverse staff members. A corporate HR team oversees initiatives in a wide range of countries and helps coordinate best practice sharing. What has been successful in one country might be a great fit in another, or it might be unique to that location. The complexity of developing Talent Management strategies and tracking results is a detailed process, but it is essential for ensuring all locations are a great place to work.

Employee Engagement and Cultural Influencers

Within the world's largest corporations are employees who face unique and overarching challenges that are oftentimes roadblocks to Engagement. However, many employees who reside in countries that have economic problems similar to those aforementioned have higher levels of Engagement than more prosperous countries.

Countries with the highest level of Engaged employees include Mexico (54 percent), Brazil (37 percent), and India (36 percent).[12] According to various reports from the World Bank, the United Nations Development Programme, and the Central Intelligence Agency, poverty rates in these countries fluctuate from population percentages in the high 20s to the low 40s.

Countries with the lowest Engagement levels include Japan (3 percent), Hong Kong (5 percent), and South Korea (8 percent). Countries in Europe that also scored low on

Engagement include Poland (9 percent), Italy (11 percent), and France (12 percent).[13] All of these countries have comparatively lower poverty rates than the most Engaged countries, with less than 20 percent living in poverty.

Although possible reasoning behind this correlation has not yet been officially uncovered, I certainly believe it relates to people feeling lucky to be employed so they can provide for themselves and their families. When work is scarce and many people are struggling to put food on the table, employees are more likely to feel appreciative of simply *having* a job. (Although managers in Mexico may be highly effective, chances are they are not the reason why employees are more Engaged in that country than any other.) Essentially, it is easier for companies in economically depressed regions to find job candidates who have a naturally Engaged disposition.

When global organizations assess their Engagement levels throughout the world, it is important to consider regional benchmarking data. This will allow for an apples-to-apples comparison and a more accurate assessment of Engagement progress and success. Adjusting Engagement strategies and catering to individual regions will allow global organizations to make a much more resounding impact on their population, thus creating a Magnetic Culture.

Corporate Social Responsibility

As discussed in Chapter 6, in the corporate landscape of today's world there are four generations of employees attempting to coexist in the workplace. The newest addition, Millennials, have a fresh viewpoint and strong set of values that affect the way they believe organizations should operate. As they hit the job market for the first time, rather than just talking about benefits and salary, as many of their older counterparts did,

Millennials are also looking for their employers to give back to their communities, reduce their carbon footprint, and be socially responsible. As a result, Corporate Social Responsibility (CSR) is becoming more popular than ever before.

In fact, CSR is often a key factor in the decision to join or stay with an organization, as well as a Key Driver of Engagement for Millennials. As this younger population establishes itself in the workforce, organizations can foster Engagement by incorporating CSR into their mission and values. CSR involves internally monitoring an organization's actions and the impact the organization has on the environment, people, and community. In addition, organizations also must observe and decrease the environmental impact of the organization, as well as educate future generations about the importance of CSR.

Two large global technology firms, Intel and EMC^2, have already embraced the importance of CSR by including CSR initiatives in their policies and missions. To better examine various CSR practices, we spoke with two passionate and dedicated employees within these organizations.

Case Study: Intel

Founded in 1968, Intel Corporation is an industry-leading technology company with locations spread around the world. Corporate Social Responsibility is extremely important to Intel's global workforce of 82,500 employees and is directly integrated into the goals of the business. Intel recognizes the impact it could have on a global level by including a worldwide focus in its CSR Strategy. *"One of the four objectives in our global strategy is 'Care for our people and our planet, and inspire the next generation,'"* said Suzanne Fallender, Director of CSR Strategy and Communications.[14] With over 14 years of experience in the field of corporate responsibility, Fallender has been a key player in developing best practices for CSR initiatives at Intel.

Intel's CSR projects are chosen based on a combination of factors. Initiatives that have a direct impact on Intel's business outcomes, such as the effect the organization's products have on the environment, are a natural fit for CSR Strategies. Intel is also constantly working to meet goals that would reduce its carbon footprint, including creating energy-efficient products and environmentally friendly office spaces, as well as encouraging recycling and water conservation. According to Fallender, Intel has become the number one voluntary purchaser of green power in the United States.

In addition to protecting the environment, Intel sponsors outreach programs to help people in need and educate future generations. Ideas for these outreach programs often stem from what the organization knows best—its products. Intel supports science and engineering fairs across the globe, educating future generations through its technology. Additionally, Intel created the "Intel Teach Program," which provides techniques to help teachers incorporate technology into their lessons. Programs that affect younger generations help build a stronger base of future workers; therefore, programs like the Intel Teach Program are vital to both organizations and our planet's future.

To ensure that Intel's employees are dedicated to CSR, a portion of each employee's compensation is linked to the achievement of CSR initiatives. There are also programs in place that reward employees for their contributions to CSR. One such program, the "Intel Environmental Excellence Awards," encourages teamwork among members by rewarding teams for environmental initiatives. The awards not only encourage employees to get involved in and promote CSR programs, but also increase cooperation among team members, contributing to another Engagement Driver.

Case Study: EMC^2

EMC^2, a global technology organization, believes Corporate Social Responsibility should have diverse objectives and be incorporated directly into an organization's goals. EMC^2 has 48,500 employees worldwide and operates in more than 80 countries. Founded in 1979, EMC^2 has 30-plus years of experience that has helped it to understand why CSR is important and to build CSR into the structure of its organization. According to Kathrin Winkler, Vice President and Chief Sustainability Officer of EMC^2, corporate initiatives at EMC^2 are organized around the three Ps: people, planet, and prosperity.[15]

EMC^2 has established several practices that help decrease the organization's direct impact on the environment, including reducing the energy used by their products and maintaining environmentally sustainable working conditions. The organization founded a "green team" consisting of individuals who ensure that products of EMC^2 have a positive impact on the environment. EMC^2 also sponsors various programs internationally to encourage children, especially underprivileged youth, to choose courses or future careers with a focus in math or science, both of which are important to the field of technology.

Other programs, perhaps not directly tied to the organization's industry, are chosen based on communication between leaders and employees. *"Our very best projects entail collaboration between the larger company and our employees,"* Winkler said. This collaboration was demonstrated by one EMC^2 employee who managed a team that repaired used computers and sent them to schools in Kenya. The employee worked with the leadership team to develop this initiative. Their approval and contribution led to successful implementation of the program. Allowing employees to contribute to CSR initiatives not only empowers them, but also allows them to feel an increased connection with the leadership team and the company itself. In addition, by listening to employees about their ideas for CSR initiatives, the leadership team shows they take employee ideas seriously and are willing to listen to employees' suggestions and concerns.

CSR also has the power to link with other important corporate values, such as education and work/life balance, as is evident by one annual contest at EMC². In this contest, employees' children create drawings illustrating how and why the environment needs protecting. Not only does the project focus on the environment, it also allows for educational outreach. In addition, the contest allows employees to spend quality time with their children, which helps to create work/life balance. *"Linking our CSR values with other values that are important to our employees allows us to connect the two with each other,"* said Winkler, indicating CSR can be very beneficial in building and sustaining Employee Engagement.

EMC² recognizes how important positive reinforcement is to the effective implementation of CSR initiatives. *"Corporate Social Responsibility should be part of a corporate culture. The more we enable [our employees], the more we will succeed,"* said Winkler. The organization holds annual "Sustainability Innovation Awards" to recognize the work employees have done throughout the year in advancing CSR objectives. Recognition through this award not only helps employees gain a sense of accomplishment, but also engages employees and keeps them excited about CSR initiatives.

Small Steps, Big Resultss

By taking small steps, any organization can begin to build strong CSR programs like those at EMC² and Intel. One best practice I recommend is to simply encourage employees to recycle by placing a recycling bin in the kitchen, or establish an all-team "Volunteer Day," where everyone works together to achieve a common goal. By recognizing how important and beneficial each employee is to the successful implementation of CSR policies, social responsibility can be greatly advanced. The connection between CSR, the organization, and the Engagement of employees is evident. Encouraging employees to become excited about and dedicated to CSR initiatives is vital to improving Engagement, particularly among the younger population. CSR can be quickly and easily integrated into the workplace, and often has phenomenal results. Through CSR, employees feel more connected and worthwhile, leading to a more engaged workforce and the potential to really make a difference in the world on a grand scale.

Progress in Engagement

Talent Management is always evolving, and it is important for organizations to continuously explore ways to advance their culture and increase Engagement. Incorporating fun into the workplace can add an intangible magnetic quality and promote employee camaraderie. Having a casual dress code can help employees be more comfortable at work and see they are trusted to make good decisions. Addressing stress management and supporting a positive work/life balance will help reduce burnout and increase your staff's overall health. A focus on multinational Engagement will ensure your organization is a good place to work for employees of all different backgrounds. Finally, CSR initiatives will show employees and customers your organization is making a positive impact that they can help support. The multitude of opportunities for improvement can be daunting at times, but progress is every Leader's best friend. As long as you are moving forward, you are going in the right direction.

Chapter 8

TAKING ACTION TOWARD ENGAGEMENT

Be the change you want to see in the world.

—MAHATMA GANDHI

It is time to end the rat race. We are humans, not rats, and every human deserves to love his or her job. If you have been thinking about and hoping to improve the culture at your organization, it's time to take action. Many leaders have a tendency to procrastinate, and that is often due to fear: *"What if people think my ideas are stupid? What if people see me fail?"* I say, *"So what?"* The consequences of not taking action are far worse than potential rejection. Obsessing over what others think of you is self-destructive behavior, and if it continues, it will likely be destructive for your organization as well. Fear is a natural human reaction; courage is a choice. Leaders must have confidence in their ideas, and the courage to take action to make them a reality.

What will attract top talent to your organization? Will it be your organization's reputation for honest open communication? Will it be the in-depth training and career advancement programs that your company offers? Will it be the workplace flexibility and a casual dress code? Or will it be the fully stocked snack pantry and the ability to bring your dog to work? Perhaps you will build a Magnetic Culture through all of the above and more. By simply focusing on Employee Engagement you will make meaningful changes that will truly impact Talent Management and, subsequently, overall success.

Developing an Engagement Strategy

Where do you start? The best way to find out the areas that are the biggest opportunities for improvement is through employee feedback. (After reading the first seven chapters of this book, I am sure this suggestion does not come as a surprise!) While everything aforementioned can be beneficial for increasing Employee Engagement, it helps to know exactly where you currently stand so you can prioritize initiatives and measure your progress. It's time to set a baseline.

A study like the Key Driver Analysis is a great way to understand exactly what factors are most impactful to your employees' Engagement and Overall Job Satisfaction. HR Solutions' Key Drivers are calculated from our entire normative database, so they represent the average across all major industries. While this is a good model to follow, your unique culture could have slightly different priorities. Variances in Key Drivers could occur for a myriad of reasons, such as the demographics of your workforce, your industry, your employees' concerns, and your organization's culture.

For example, through an Employee Engagement Survey and Key Driver Analysis, you might uncover that Key Driver 4, Strategy and Mission, is actually the most important Engagement Driver to your staff. This could occur at a nonprofit organization that attracts employees who are passionate about the organization's cause above all else. Such a staff is likely to have slightly different Engagement priorities than employees in other industries who feel less personally connected to the organization's overall mission.

At another organization, a Key Driver Analysis might uncover that Key Driver 9, Availability of Resources to Perform the Job Effectively, is the top Engagement Driver. This could occur at an organization where employees rely heavily on tools or equipment to earn compensation, such as taxi drivers who need reliable vehicles and working credit card machines to earn tips. The direct link between resources and potential earnings would make this driver a top Engagement priority.

When it comes down to it, each organization is different, and each organization's Magnetic Culture will naturally be different as well. The key to success is finding out exactly what is important to your team, prioritizing, and action planning to make it a reality.

It is extremely important for leaders to make a constant effort to build magnetism at their organization, even during times of success. Many of the companies highlighted in Jim Collins's book, *Good to Great: Why Some Companies Make the Leap . . . and Others Don't*, experienced troubling times after years of extreme success, including Fannie Mae, which has since been bailed out by the U.S. government. There will always be companies out there that are making progress. If you aren't making progress as well, you will be left behind.

Developing a Recognition Program

Recognition is Key Driver 1. As stated in Chapter 3, a strong Recognition program can be the difference maker in an Engaged workforce. In fact, it boosts Engagement by 35 percent.[1] Managers should create a program where incentives are aligned to elicit the desired behavior. To help simplify this process, we have compiled a list of 10 best practices for developing an organizational culture of Recognition.

Best Practice 1: Define What Should Be Recognized

When establishing a Recognition program, it is important for an organization to define the behaviors or outcomes that are deemed worthy of Recognition. A great way to develop a guideline is for senior leadership to brainstorm a list of employee actions that contribute to the organization's success and mission. Ideas can range from bringing in a certain amount of revenue, to receiving a positive comment from a customer, to simply volunteering to help a coworker. This list should be shared with all managers and used as a guideline for giving Recognition.

Management can also create a "chance points" program using a list of Recognition-worthy actions. Employees track their own efforts and earn points through their actions. At the end of the month, each point turns into a raffle ticket to win a prize.

When the desired actions or outcomes are clearly defined, employee Recognition can be streamlined throughout the organization, helping to create an electric culture of Recognition.

Best Practice 2: Be Sincere

All too often, companies turn Recognition programs into just another task that needs regular attention. Employees can tell when a manager just "goes through the motions" of providing Recognition, but has lost interest in showing genuine appreciation for staff members' efforts. This lack of sincerity and enthusiasm can make Recognition diminish in meaning, even if the reward remains the same. The reason that Recognition is so powerful is because people thrive on the warm fuzzy feeling of being appreciated. If sincere appreciation is lost from a Recognition program, it will no longer be effective.

Best Practice 3: Recognize in Public and in Private

Public and private Recognition can be appropriate in different situations, and the best results come from employing both methods. Public Recognition is highly effective because it gives employees structure so they know what to expect. If top performing employees are recognized at each monthly meeting, employees have a goal they can work toward. For many employees, being congratulated in front of peers can actually be the most rewarding aspect of receiving praise. Alternately, it is important for managers to keep in mind that not all people like to be the center of attention. For individuals with a meek or introverted demeanor, having all eyes suddenly turn to them in a public meeting might be painfully embarrassing. To praise employees who do not like to be in the spotlight, public Recognition should be toned down so it does not end up actually hindering their Engagement.

Providing private Recognition can also be very effective in showing employees they are appreciated. Private Recognition is easier for managers to give more frequently, and it is as simple as a quick "on-the-spot" verbal thank you. Whether it is an e-mail, voice mail, handwritten note, or just stopping by in person, letting employees know that they have done a good job goes a long way and only takes a few moments.

Best Practice 4: Balance the Criticism

Criticism is an important factor that affects employee perception of Recognition. Unfortunately, it can be common for employees to focus on the criticism they received rather than the Recognition. With that in mind, managers should not shy away from providing constructive feedback because they are afraid it will hurt an employee's feelings. Managers should, however, be aware of how criticism can adversely affect an employee's perception of Recognition efforts overall.

A common word that managers use when giving feedback is *but*. When you tell an employee, "You did a great job on the vast majority of this project, *but* . . ." it has the effect of causing the employee to forget the first part of your sentence. Oftentimes, people get upset with themselves for making mistakes, and they tend to focus on the shortcomings you have illuminated, rather than any positive feedback you may have provided. Separating positive feedback from suggestions for improvement (even just in separate sentences) is more effective in getting the proper message across.

If a manager has been providing more constructive criticism than usual, it could be a good idea to balance the criticism by increasing Recognition efforts when the employee performs well. As a general rule, constructive criticism is best used to help employees improve performance, not Engagement.

Best Practice 5: When in Doubt, Ask!

The type of Recognition or reward is not a benefit if the person does not want it. It is unwise to assume all employees want the same things. Ask individual employees how they would like to be recognized. Although this is the most straightforward approach, oftentimes managers overlook the simplicity of open communication with employees. Telling employees you want to recognize them in a way that is meaningful to them shows genuine interest and appreciation in advance, which is a great first step in providing effective Recognition.

Best Practice 6: Equal Does Not Necessarily Mean Fair

Employee Recognition does not have to be equal. To make Recognition meaningful, it needs to be *appropriate* for the effort or accomplishment. In a perfect world, all employees would be equally dedicated and successful, but in reality, it is unlikely that will happen. Organizations will generally have certain employees who consistently outperform others. If managers do not fairly recognize and reward these special employees, they will go elsewhere.

When I first started HR Solutions, I didn't create bonus metrics; instead I determined the bonuses subjectively. The people who got the best bonuses had jaw-dropping experiences when they learned the dollar amount, and had absolutely no complaints. The people who got lower bonuses had an immediate inclination to grab onto the *F* word: *favoritism.* The first time someone accused me of this, I looked at the underperforming employee (who deserved a low bonus) and said, *"You're right. I do have favorites. My favorite employees are passionately engaged in their jobs and their performance results in supreme excellence and stellar customer service outcomes."* This instantly muted the criticism.

When the organization grew, we had to switch to a more socialist method of determining bonuses. The change caused some of my "favorite" employees to leave, likely because they thought others who didn't come near them in performance were being rewarded with bonuses they didn't deserve. Having clear bonus metrics in place was good for ensuring that employees knew what to expect based on their performance. However, I've gotten the best results from generously rewarding top performers.

To cut back on perceptions of favoritism, top performers can be rewarded more frequently in private. Making employee Recognition equal is a risk that is not worth taking.

Best Practice 7: Do Not Overdo It

Although employees can thrive on Recognition, it is possible to have too much of a good thing. Over-recognizing can quickly dilute the meaning and heighten the risk of seeming insincere to employees. In addition, if employees are congratulated for every single task they complete, they could have little motivation to work harder or do a better job. In essence, just like many good things in life, it is best not to overindulge.

Best Practice 8: Determine Appropriate Rewards

Rewards and gifts are the cherry on top of Recognition. While not always necessary, it can be a great addition to simply telling employees they have done a great job. With that in mind, the reward must be *appropriate* for the action or outcome. Giving a reward that is disproportionately smaller than the amount of time or effort expended can actually decrease the value of Recognition, and possibly serve as a de-motivator.

Best Practice 9: Educate Employees on Your Recognition Efforts

It is important for employees to understand the importance that their organization places on Recognition and the effort managers undertake to ensure that employees are recognized. For example, if managers are privately rewarding employees with gift cards or extra paid time off (PTO) for a job well done, all staff members should be made aware of those initiatives, but they do not need to know who received what. Managers can simply state *X* number of gift cards were given out in February, as well as *X* number of "Leave Early Passes." When employees see the whole picture of actions taken to help increase their Recognition and Engagement, they are much more likely to have a positive viewpoint on the Recognition they receive.

A best practice for involving employees is to ask for feedback on new initiatives they would like to see. Any changes that are made as a result of employee feedback should be clearly communicated to staff members.

Best Practice 10: Encourage Employees to Recognize One Another

To create a true culture of Recognition, everyone should be involved. While senior leadership should manage organizational Recognition efforts, employees should be encouraged to recognize their colleagues' hard work as well. A best practice for involving employees is to post a whiteboard in a high-traffic area where employees can publicly recognize each other. HR Solutions has seen a great response from employees through the implementation of our "Snaps Board." Employees regularly write on this whiteboard to congratulate one another on efforts and accomplishments. This idea can also be translated to a virtual environment through an internal intranet system. Management could also dedicate a few minutes of team meetings for employees to thank their colleagues who have recently gone above and beyond.

Recognition as Second Nature

Luckily, it is easy for managers to begin increasing Recognition immediately. A great way to start a new initiative is by setting a calendar reminder to recognize one employee each day, and increasing this number over time. Another option is to pay it forward: tell employees that each time someone thanks them, they should thank two other people. This simple concept will increase Recognition exponentially, helping everyone understand the true power of a *thank you*. When providing frequent Recognition becomes second nature, Employee

Engagement should increase as well, creating a workplace culture headed toward organizational success.[2]

The Path of Career Development

Advancing within the organization is a major Driver of Engagement. It is wise to have a "layer-cake" model that allows employees room to grow and advance through promotions. For example, an organization could have various levels of a certain position, such as associate project managers, project managers, and senior project managers. When employees get a strong command of the tasks associated with their current position, they are eligible for a promotion to the next level of project manager. The change in title and bump in salary are conducive to supporting Engagement. Organizations, large and small, can use this strategy to capitalize on Engagement Driver 2: Career Development.

Encourage Leadership

The opportunity to lead a group of people or spearhead a project is great experience for employees. As a best practice, organizations should allow all employees the opportunity to manage different projects. Whether it is organizing a major companywide initiative, or simply organizing a team lunch, being the point person on a project gives employees the chance to show off their leadership skills, as well as gain experience coordinating with multiple people.

In organizations with a flat structure, especially associations and many nonprofits, appointing leaders for projects or teams is a great way to engage employees through Career Development opportunities. Managers should be sure to acknowledge when employees have done a great job being a project or team leader, as this inextricably ties the top two Engagement Drivers together—Recognition and Career Development.

Action Planning

- Brainstorm the projects that do not currently have a leader or point person. There is a good chance it would be beneficial to assign someone to manage these anyway. Try to spread out new responsibilities, so multiple employees benefit.
- Select projects that employees could take turns managing. Allowing people to volunteer for leading these initiatives is a great way to offer the opportunity to those who want more responsibility without overwhelming those who are already very busy. It also promotes a sense of fairness in Leadership opportunities.
- Ask some more tenured employees if they have projects they would like to hand off to someone else. As employees gain experience and take on more projects, the more elemental tasks could be transitioned to employees whose skills are less advanced. This opportunity gives experienced staff the time to work on harder assignments, while newer staff members can take pride in managing their own initiatives.

Certifications

A great way to promote Career Development opportunities for employees is to offer internal certifications for core competencies. Doing so also shows customers that employees are properly trained and fully prepared to give great service. Certifications allow employees to work toward goals without changing positions.

Many industries offer certifications. Hairstylists often earn color certification to show their proficiency in color-treating hair. Automotive organizations offer certifications that show employees are knowledgeable on auto maintenance and repair. Restaurants oftentimes certify staff on their knowledge of legal alcohol consumption (in some states by law, in others by choice).

Action Planning

There are many possibilities for incorporating certification into staff education and training.

- Think about where internal certifications could fit into your organization. Would all employees benefit from an onboarding certification? Could you offer certifications that are necessary for managing more advanced tasks, or helping customers with specific issues? If you already offer internal certifications, how could that program become more enhanced?
- Determine which well-respected industry certifications would be beneficial to your employees. For Human Resources professionals, the industry standard certifications are PHR, SPHR, and GPHR certifications. Employers should create a plan to help employees study and apply for professional certifications, such as these.
- Create employee incentives for earning a certification (outside of the realm of Career Development). Raises, bonuses, Recognition, and special privileges or parties are all great options.
- Market the certification offerings to customers. Information should be on the company website and any promotions for the commitment to customer service. In addition, consider using advertisements, social

media, and, if applicable, in-store promotions to market certification programs. Employee bios and media kits should include certifications. Employees who interact with customers in certain industries could also wear something to signify their certification level, such as a button or sticker on their name tag.

- Actively market the certification program to current employees and potential employees, and educate them on the benefits. Promoting this information is key to the success of the program. If no one knows about certification offerings or thinks they are of value, it will not help attract, engage, or retain employees.

Educational Advancement

Certain industries, such as those that are focused on business, are often at constant risk of losing less tenured employees who choose to pursue a graduate degree, such as a master of business administration (MBA). If higher positions within a company require a higher degree (which is very often the case), lower-ranking employees will perceive they are unlikely to advance in their career within the organization without going back to school. Employees who are considering higher education are the people who are intrinsically motivated and have a strong desire to advance themselves personally and professionally. In other words, these are likely to be an organization's most actively engaged employees, the ones you really do not want to lose.

Essentially, engaged employees who are considering higher education have four choices:

1. Leave their organization and go back to school full time.
2. Leave their organization to work somewhere else that offers Career Development without an advanced degree.

3. Stay with their organization without going back to school, and stay "stuck" in the same position until they are no longer engaged employees.
4. Stay with their organization, go back to school part time, and earn a degree and subsequent promotion.

Losing star employees because they choose to enter full-time education programs (Option 1) can be a costly Talent Management casualty. Helping employees cover the expenses of continued education is a win-win solution for employers and their employees alike, a "no-brainer" of sorts. Organizations that educate their staff and support them on climbing the internal advancement ladder will bolster Engagement through Career Development.

Option 4 is the only one that is good for employers that aspire to build a Magnetic Culture. Hence, many organizations have their cards stacked against them. It can be very smart for organizations to develop a plan that entices top talent into choosing to go back to school part time. The most effective way of doing this is through tuition reimbursement, or tuition assistance. While programs vary greatly depending on the organization, the goal is to make the program enough of a benefit that employees actually use it.

Tuition Reimbursement/Assistance Basics

Some basics of tuition reimbursement and tuition assistance include:

- Many programs are only available to employees who have been with the organization for a certain amount of time, such as one year. This policy ensures employees have proven to be a good fit with the company before receiving such a generous benefit from their employer. Another approach is to offer tuition reimbursement from the very beginning of employment as a method for attracting motivated employees who are interested in going back to school part time.

- There should be a contract that requires an employee stay on staff for a certain number of months, or years, after her education is complete, or she forfeits any financial assistance from her employer. This precaution serves as an insurance policy, preventing employees from getting their education on their employer's dime and resigning before that organization sees a return on investment. To combat legality issues, oftentimes organizations issue tuition reimbursement as a "loan," which serves as legal protection.
- Courses should be "work related" to be eligible for reimbursement. While this requirement falls into a gray area, it will ensure a banking organization isn't paying for classes on ceramics. Approving courses or degrees that qualify for financial assistance can be the responsibility of an HR professional.
- Some programs pay out different amounts based on the grade employees earn in each class. Oftentimes, a C grade or lower will not qualify for reimbursement from an employer. While this can help motivate employees to study hard, it can also lead to added stress in a situation where work/life balance is already a challenge.

Case Study: LinkedIn

Many people are familiar with LinkedIn as a professional networking website and a resource for posting and applying to job openings. What people may not know is that the company is also a great place to work. Launched in 2003, LinkedIn has magnetically attracted over 100 million users, spanning more than 200 countries and territories worldwide. This level of growth can, in large part, be attributed to a strong pool of talented individuals.

LinkedIn offers a dynamic, innovative culture that focuses on employee education. *"We motivate people with opportunity and self-improvement,"* said Mike Gamson, Senior Vice President of Global Sales at LinkedIn.[3] He described the amount of individual opportunity that is available to employees of LinkedIn as being endless. *"When someone joins our team, we are invested in their passions and dreams instantly,"* said Gamson. *"One of our biggest missions is to help our employees be more productive and successful in everything they strive to accomplish."*

Senior leaders at LinkedIn consider the organization to be an educational institution for employees, and they make it a top priority to help employees be successful in everything they strive to accomplish. LinkedIn recognizes that employees will leave the company through natural attrition, and they do not shy away from the topic. Uniquely, senior leaders focus on helping employees fulfill their potential so they are prepared for the next phase of their career, even if it is with another organization.

LinkedIn understands the force of a Magnetic Culture through its online platform. As a member of LinkedIn, users are prompted to connect with colleagues and friends. As more and more people join, the magnetic pull gets stronger. The Talent Management philosophy of LinkedIn works the same way; people want to work at LinkedIn because they want to be part of the culture. Senior leaders understand that it is a competitive world out there and employees want to make money, but they have actively seen how culture impacts Engagement and trumps compensation.

Gamson thinks HR Solutions' Key Drivers of Engagement are spot-on. He emphasizes the importance of Driver Number 4 at LinkedIn: Strategy and Mission—especially the Freedom and Autonomy to Succeed and Contribute to the Organization's Success. Employees at LinkedIn believe they can transform themselves, the company, and even the world through their work. Considering the success of LinkedIn in altering the course of recruiting, professional networking, and Talent Management, the employees are certainly right.

Tying Feedback to Your Bottom Line

Are there cost-savings opportunities that your organization has overlooked? If so, chances are that employees have already identified some of them. Unfortunately, not many organizations actively ask employees for their feedback on this important topic. As one organization recently proved, including employees in cost-savings initiatives can not only be profitable, it can impact Employee Engagement as well.

Case Study: How Employee Feedback Can Directly Impact Your Bottom Line

Northeast Hospital Corporation (NHC), which represents several acute care hospitals in Massachusetts, recently conducted an Employee Engagement Survey with HR Solutions and included this survey item:

> *"There are cost-savings opportunities in my department that have not been taken advantage of by this organization."*

Upon receiving feedback that many employees felt there were untapped opportunities to cut expenses, NHC launched the "My Cost-Savings Idea (My CSI)" program. The program encourages employees to submit an idea that could save NHC money. To ensure employees are motivated to participate in the program and to recognize them for their efforts, approved ideas garner employees a monetary award.

Since the program began two years ago, NHC employees have generated cost-savings ideas totaling over $250,000, a substantial figure for a young program. As a result of these ideas, NHC generously awarded the staff who made the suggestions more than $7,000.

"The 'My CSI' program has been a huge success," said Althea C. Lyons, Vice President of Human Resources and Development at NHC. *"By sharing cost-savings ideas, our employees are making a profound, lasting impact as well as demonstrating their continued commitment to our organization."*[4]

The following are some of the creative ideas submitted by NHC employees.

Human Resources

An NHC employee came up with the idea to end the employee referral program due to the country's high unemployment rate. The employee felt it was no longer a viable method to get quality referrals. Savings, on an annual basis, was $44,000; the employee was awarded $2,000 for the idea.

Nonphysician Medical Practitioners

Two NHC employees proposed the idea to discontinue mailings and faxes to nonphysician medical practitioners because the information was already submitted electronically. This idea resulted in an annual savings of $9,000; each employee was awarded $225 for the idea.

Pharmacy and Respiratory

Two NHC employees partnered to develop a new patient-specific assessment protocol for dry powder inhalers. Each patient's ability to properly use a dry powder inhaler is now evaluated by a respiratory therapist prior to dispensing and charging the inhaler. This new evidence-based assessment reduces waste and provides better patient care. The annual savings was $18,819.96; each employee received $235 for the idea.

Surgical Services

An NHC employee had the idea to switch from a disposable product in the operating room to a nondisposable product that would not need to be purchased as frequently. This switch resulted in an annual savings of $63,408 and also improved clinician satisfaction; the employee was awarded $2,000 for the idea.

Bottom Line and Employee Engagement

The aforementioned cost-savings ideas and others like them are having a direct impact on both NHC's bottom line and Employee Engagement. By empowering employees to suggest ideas that result in positive business outcomes, the staff understands how they can *directly* contribute to the success of the organization. This is certainly a best practice, and NHC has set an example for employers in all industries.[5]

Feeding Coworker Satisfaction

Culture is comprised of many elements, but the driving factor is people. As an employer, you can get the right people on the bus, but how they interact during the ride is just as important. While you cannot control personal interactions between employees, you *can* create an environment that promotes positive interactions. Since relationships with coworkers are often the glue that binds employees to their organization, it behooves employers to help build coworker camaraderie.

Eighty-seven percent of people think their coworkers are friendly and helpful.[6] This is one of the most positive responses out of all job-related survey items. Employers can feed Coworker Satisfaction by providing opportunities for employees to interact and get to know each other. Supporting this type of social interaction should not be considered a waste of time, as it directly supports Engagement. In addition, when employees get to know one another, they will likely be able to communicate more effectively to complete projects. Improved communication between team members leads to higher quality and productivity, which ties directly to your bottom line.

Case Study: Talent Management Success Is "M'mm-M'mm Good"

Red and white. Chicken noodle. Andy Warhol. What do these things all have in common? If you guessed the Campbell Soup Company, you hit the nail right on the head. The fact that I can provide a list of four seemingly unrelated things and it is still possible to identify what I am alluding to points to the iconic brand that Campbell's has created.

Since 1869, Campbell Soup Company has made a name for itself in the food world, now reaching customers in 120 countries. With over 18,000 employees and nearly $8 billion in sales of soup, juice, and baked snack choices, the company has established itself as a leader in its industry.

What makes Campbell Soup Company such a successful organization? According to Denise Morrison, President and CEO of Campbell Soup Company, it is having all employees contribute to building and sustaining a diverse, inclusive, engaged, and socially responsible workplace focused on delivering business results with integrity and high Employee Engagement, resulting in high performance. Named to her role on August 1, 2011, Morrison is working from a strong foundation built by her predecessor, Doug Conant, who created a culture structured around the *"belief that business results start with the culture and your people."*[7] Essentially, Campbell's success in the marketplace and the community starts with Talent Management in the workplace. As such, Campbell has made engaging, aka "nourishing," employees a top priority.

Senior Leaders at Campbell do all they can to make the organization feel like a community to its employees. Despite the company's large size, employees rarely feel lost in the shuffle. *"[One] thing that makes Campbell unique is that we are a large company . . . that actually feels like a small company,"* said Jackie Scanlan, Vice President of Global Talent Management and Organization Effectiveness at Campbell Soup Company. Employees are encouraged to intermingle with individuals on all levels. The company constantly stresses that all employees should be encouraged to interact with each other and that everyone's opinions should be heard, regardless of their level within the company. The closeness and dialogue between all levels contributes to the small company feel.

Encouraging interactions among staff members can lead to frequent interruptions, but in his tenure at Campbell, Conant encouraged team members to view so-called interruptions differently from other organizations. Instead of trying to minimize interactions, Conant advised employees to view these conversations as a way to solve problems, build relationships, and drive success. He referred to these moments as "touchpoints," which encourage active listening and conversing, so as to truly get the most out of every conversation. As a result of these "touchpoints" and follow-up dialogues, employees will have a greater likelihood of feeling heard and leadership will have a better understanding about what is going on in the workplace. A larger sense of community will naturally develop within an organization. Interruptions are rarely unavoidable, but if handled effectively, can actually help corporations.

Campbell Soup Company also uses its brand in creative ways to establish an association between the organization and its employees, thus driving Engagement. The brand is so recognizable, it is easy to tie the products into the identity of the workplace, said Scanlan. In keeping with this idea, meeting rooms in Campbell's headquarters relate to the brand, with names such as "Margaret Rudkin" (the founder of Pepperidge Farm) and "Red and White." Scanlan pointed out, "*We try to have fun with the names, and employees identify with it.*"[8] Incorporating the brand into life within the organization increases the connection employees have and keeps them engaged in an inspired manner.

As CEO, Morrison will ensure that Campbell continues to focus on delivering business results by maintaining a diverse, inclusive, and engaged workforce. By putting people first in its recipe for success, Campbell's has created a culture that really is "m'mm-m'mm good."

The Little Things

You would be amazed at the impact of seemingly inconsequential initiatives. Over the years, I have learned to go with my employees' suggestions, no matter how minor. However, this was not always the case. Several years back, we received one write-in comment on our Employee Engagement Survey that we should offer doughnuts at our monthly meetings. I thought about it briefly, and nixed the idea because I didn't relate to the desire for doughnuts at work. People could eat breakfast at home or bring food with them, just like any other day. The following year, we received 10 write-in comments on our Employee Survey that we should offer doughnuts at our monthly meetings. Again, I decided against it, thinking it simply wasn't necessary. I am embarrassed to say it took me three years in a row of receiving the same feedback on the desire for doughnuts at meetings for me to actually take the suggestion seriously and buy the doughnuts.

When I finally did approve the "doughnut budget" for our meetings, our Leadership Team decided that a different volunteer each month could handle the responsibility. The staff's reaction was akin to Moses parting the Red Sea. Employees felt empowered by the opportunity to plan breakfast for their colleagues. One person even went so far as to make bacon for the entire staff before work and bring it in. Employees started to look forward to our meeting days, simply because we provided breakfast.

I was honestly shocked that this small change had such a resounding impact. It was a great lesson: how just because something isn't important to you doesn't mean it isn't important to other people. Turning our meetings into breakfast meetings has certainly added an element of fun into our culture and showed employees we care about their suggestions, which has been much more impactful than I ever anticipated.

Pet-Friendly Workplaces

Bringing your dog to work was virtually unheard of 20 years ago, but not today. For many animal enthusiasts, a pet-friendly workplace might just be the difference maker in how an organizational culture can be head and shoulders above the rest. Employees and employers alike can benefit from the addition of a workplace pet.

Cost Savings for Employees

The doggy day care/dog walking business is booming due to employees working long hours. Since many dogs cannot make it through the day without a "bathroom" break, employees are often faced with the choice of paying someone else to take care of their dog, or leaving work early to do it themselves.

Thirty-nine percent of American households own at least one dog.[9] For employees with four-legged friends, bringing Fido to work can save a great deal of money, while also increasing hours on the job. In addition, if your organization is unable to compensate employees as generously as you would like, due to budget constraints, saving employees money in other areas certainly contributes to the total value of the position.

An Increase in Overall Wellness

Having pets in the workplace encourages employees to do something active during their breaks, such as going for walks or playing fetch. Spending time with an animal can add an instant boost to an employee's mood, increasing productivity after the break is over.

Stress in the workplace can pose a significant threat to employees' health. According to the Centers for Disease Control, simply being around a cat or dog can decrease stress levels, and petting a cat or dog has been shown to reduce blood pressure. Pet ownership has also been linked to lower cholesterol and lower triglyceride levels, which minimizes the risk of stroke and heart disease.

If having dogs or cats in the workplace is out of the question, fish have been known to help people relax as well. Watching fish swim in a tank can have a calming effect on employees and customers, as well as contribute to the office's ambiance.

Camaraderie

From dogs to goldfish, animals present an opportunity for employees to socialize and have fun in the workplace. Pets also create a heightened sense of community, where staff members are collectively committed to caring for the well-being of the office pet.

Creating a Customer Experience

Many people love animals. I bet you've visited a business where a mellow cat was relaxing behind the counter or a dog roamed freely, enjoying the ear scratchings he received from customers. This is the type of element that makes an organization unique and gets customers to come back.

Companionship and Safety

For employees who work alone or with very few coworkers, having a pet at work can help decrease loneliness. Companionship can make employees feel more comfortable and focused. In addition, a larger dog can increase safety for employees who work in isolated areas.

Benefits of Pet Policies

When considering pet policies, it is important to think about the organization's desired culture, environment, and employees. In some workplaces, it may not be feasible due to the nature of the industry, staff allergies, or restrictions by workforce property management. Each organization is different and should have a pet policy that caters to its specific needs. Creating a policy that will allow animals into the office may present some unique challenges, but will ultimately allow both employees and employers to see a number of benefits resulting in positive employee morale.

What's Important to Your Team?

As shown throughout this chapter, many different actions, big and small, can be taken toward creating a more engaged workforce. Focusing on Employee Engagement to build a Magnetic Culture will not only help attract top talent, but also reinvigorate your current employees. Whether you are able to help employees move forward in their careers through educational opportunities or simply make their day-to-day work life more rewarding through small initiatives, you must find out what is important to your employees and work it into the cultural fabric of your organization.

THE ULTIMATE SUMMIT: ENGAGEMENT

Being an avid mountaineer, I can't help but to see the parallels in high-altitude mountaineering and business: success is a constant climb. If you stop trying to move forward, you will fall behind. In both mountaineering and Talent Management, training and preparation are critical to successfully reaching the summit, or peak, of Engagement. Without proper training, there are multitudinous opportunities for Disengagement, despair, and failure in achieving one's objectives.

From the outset of the climb, or building Engagement, you need to set a clearly defined goal: a Strategy and Mission. That goal is not only measured by how high the summit is, but, most important, the dual objective of getting down and off the mountain safely. This is where the infamous Mount Everest climbers set themselves up for disaster in 1996. If they didn't reach the peak by a certain time, they agreed that the only safe option was to turn back. When that time came and they weren't at the summit, some of the climbers turned around, but others did not. They didn't stick to their plan as a team, and many perished because of it. In business, all managers and employees must agree to follow the Strategy and Mission, the overarching plan.

It is imperative to have the right tools and resources for both mountaineering and Engagement. If you head up a mountain without the proper UV sunglasses, you are at risk of going "snow-blind," which would make the summit impossible to reach, and constitute as a total failure. The same is true in business; without possessing the necessary tools and knowledge, you might as well be blind. Going blind affects your whole team as well. In mountaineering, not only does this failure ruin your climb, but also the climbs of your fellow team members, since they would need to turn around and guide you down the mountain. In business, lack of proper tools is detrimental to individuals' progress and productivity. There isn't a great Employee Engagement Survey out there that doesn't cover resources to do the job, as it is an essential aspect to organizational success.

In both mountaineering and Talent Management, teamwork makes the difference in reaching the summit. You would never begin a high-altitude mountaineering expedition with disengaged people who don't care; they will be a danger to you and everyone else. On high-altitude glacial expeditions where there is a risk of crevasse fall, climbers are literally roped together to protect one another from falling. If a climber slips, everyone else feels the tug of the person moving in the wrong direction, and the team instantly reacts by digging their pick axes into the mountain to act as an anchor. Through teamwork, they are able to pull the distressed climber back on track. In the workplace, employees and employers need to rope together *figuratively* through offering support, good communication, and genuine effort for improving Engagement.

Employees who are disengaged will refuse to participate in supporting the group's effort, and will therefore be detrimental to progress and success. We have the ability to pick our fellow climbers, or coworkers, and that is why Best-in-Class organizations do not tolerate Disengagement in the workplace; it is truly a hazard for everyone.

Figure C.1 Kevin Sheridan climbing Mt. Elbrus, Russia (elevation, 18,150 ft.)

The Mount Everest disaster might never have had happened if leaders from the climbing teams had encouraged feedback from their team members. Survivors recounted how leaders specifically told the team not to share dissenting opinions on the final push up the mountain. Survivors did in fact have a different viewpoint on the team's best direction, and that was back down the mountain. (This is where many ended up heading, without their leaders.) In climbing and in business, getting feedback from other informed team members, *especially* in high-stakes decisions, can save your life, literally or figuratively.

My grandma always said the key to a long life is to keep moving and have fun. In fact, instead of saying goodbye to people, she told them to simply, "Have fun." Our family always admired the wisdom in her unique parting phrase. She lived to the ripe old age of 92, so she can certainly be considered an expert on living a full life.

I use her advice every day; I get off my ass, make an effort to be productive, and I don't forget to have fun. This translates perfectly to building a Magnetic Culture: to be truly successful, you will have to work for it, but you and your employees should enjoy yourselves along the way.

I truly hope you have found this book to be interesting, practical, actionable, and, most important, motivating. You have the power to make meaningful, if not profound, changes at your organization, and now you are armed with the knowledge and best practices to take action. Creating a culture where Engaged employees stay and thrive is the indisputable difference maker in overall success.

Have fun.

NOTES

Chapter 1

1. HR Solutions' National Normative Database, https://actionpro.hrsolutionsinc.com (normative items; accessed May 25, 2011).
2. Ibid.
3. Jan Brockway, "Driving Employee Engagement through Performance Management," Workscape webcast, September 16, 2009, https://workscapeevents.webex.com/ec0605lb/eventcenter/recording/recordAction.do?siteurl=workscapeevents&theAction=poprecord&ecFlag=true&recordID=1577627.
4. Philip Kotler et al., *Principles of Marketing*, 2nd ed. (London: Prentice Hall Europe, 1999), 483.
5. Fredrik Abildtrup. "23 Facts about Customer Loyalty and Customer Satisfaction." *Return on Behavior Magazine*, http://www.returnonbehaviormagazine.com/articles-of-interest/23-facts-about-customer-loyalty-and-customer-satisfaction-2.html. (accessed May 6, 2011).
6. Ibid.
7. Jim Collins, *Good to Great: Why Some Companies Make the Leap . . . and Others Don't.* (New York: HarperCollins, 2001).
8. Hand washing regulations vary by organization. For the purpose of this study, hand washing compliance was defined as washing hands before and after contact with a patient. Hand washing rates were self-reported by health care professionals.
9. Centers for Disease Control and Prevention, "Preventing Healthcare-Associated Infections," CDC at Work, http://www.cdc.gov/washington/cdcatWork/pdf/infections.pdf. (accessed May 25, 2011).

Chapter 2

1. Amelia Forczak and Kevin Sheridan, "Engagement Model," *Sales & Service Excellence*, July 2010, 6.
2. HR Solutions, Inc., "Who Do You Think Should Be Primarily Responsible for Employee Engagement?" HR Solutions' website, www.hrsolutionsinc.com (accessed September 2009; no longer available). A total of 263 people completed the online poll.
3. HR Solutions, Inc. PEER Pulse demographics. From August 2009–May 2011, approximately 50,000 employees have chosen to take PEER.
4. HR Solutions' National Normative Database, https://actionpro.hrsolutionsinc.com (normative items accessed May 25, 2011).
5. Ashley Nuese, "Do You Take Your Employer to Be Your Loyal, Committed Partner? I Do," *HR Solutions eNews*, February 2011, http://www.hrsolutionsinc.com/enews_0211/Employer_Commitment_0211.html.

Chapter 3

1. HR Solutions' National Normative Database, https://actionpro.hrsolutionsinc.com (normative items; accessed May 25, 2011).
2. E-mail interview with Dan Pink, May 4, 2011.
3. Ibid.
4. Reprinted with permission from the American Society for Healthcare Human Resources Administration (ASHHRA). Amelia Forczak, "Recognition: The Key Driver of Employee Engagement," *ASHHRA e-News Brief*, April 12, 2011, http://www.naylornetwork.com/ahh-nwl/articles/index-v2.asp?aid=141503&issueID=22503.
5. Raghuram Rajan and Julie Wulf, "The Flattening Firm: From Panel Data on the Changing Nature of Corporate Hierarchies," *Review of Economics and Statistics* 88 (November 4, 2006): 759–73.
6. HR Solutions, Inc., "What Kind of Educational Advancement Opportunities Does Your Company Offer?" HR Solutions' website, http://www.hrsolutionsinc.com/hrspoll/results.cfm?QuestionID=28 (accessed May 2010). A total of 64 people completed the online poll.
7. HR Solutions' National Normative Database, https://actionpro.hrsolutionsinc.com. (normative items; accessed May 25, 2011).

8. Ibid.
9. Interview with Frits van Paasschen, July 25, 2011.
10. Reprinted with permission from AHA Solutions. Amelia Forczak, "AtlantiCare Encourages Employees to 'Get Engaged,'" *AHA Solutions eNewsletter*, July 2010, http://www.aha-solutions.org/aha-solutions/content/HR/HR/AtlantiCare_Case_Study.pdf.
11. Interview with Susan Young, April 13, 2011.
12. HR Solutions' National Normative Database, https://actionpro.hrsolutionsinc.com. (normative items; accessed May 25, 2011).
13. Ibid.
14. Ibid.
15. Bureau of Labor Statistics, "An Overview of U.S. Occupational Employment and Wages in 2009," U.S. Department of Labor, Bureau of Labor Statistics, June 2010, http://www.bls.gov/oes/highlight_2009.pdf. (accessed June 10, 2011).
16. Joe Hadzima, "How Much Does an Employee Cost," *Boston Business Journal*, 2005, http://enterpriseforum.mit.edu/mindshare/startingup/employee-cost.html. (accessed February 24, 2011).

Chapter 4

1. Judy Enns, Executive Vice President of HR Solutions/Eastridge Administrative Services.
2. Interview with Russ Laraway, June 27, 2011.
3. H.R. Solutions/Eastridge Administrative Services.
4. Francois Dufour, "Employee Referrals and LinkedIn Recruiter Emerge as Top Sources of Hire," LinkedIn Talent Advantage, June 2, 2009, http://talent.linkedin.com/blog/index.php/2009/06/employee-referrals-and-linkedin-recruiter-top-sources-of-hire (accessed June 24, 2011).
5. HR Solutions/Eastridge Administrative Services.
6. HR Solutions' National Normative Database, https://actionpro.hrsolutionsinc.com (normative items; accessed May 25, 2011). HR Solutions' "Engagement Statistics by Tenure," January 2008–May 2009.
7. Fredric D. Frank, Richard P. Finnegan, and Craig R. Taylor, "The Race for Talent: Retaining and Engaging Workers in the 21st Century," *Human Resource Planning*, September 1, 2004, http://www.commerce.uct.ac.za/Managementstudies/

Courses/BUS5033W/2008/Anton%20Schlechter/20080908/the%20race%20for%20talent%20retaining%20and%20engaging%20worksers%20in%20the%2021st%20century.pdf (accessed June 14, 2011).
8. HR Solutions' Research Institute, Exit Survey Data. The survey item is "I have thought of resigning in the last six months."
9. HR Solutions' National Normative Database, https://actionpro.hrsolutionsinc.com (normative items; accessed May 25, 2011).

Chapter 5

1. WorldatWork, "Compensation Programs and Practices," September 2010, http://www.worldatwork.org/waw/adimLink?id=42294 (accessed July 28, 2011).
2. HR Solutions' Research Institute, Exit Survey Data. The survey item is "I have thought of resigning in the last six months."
3. HR Solutions' National Normative Database, https://actionpro.hrsolutionsinc.com (normative items; accessed May 25, 2011).
4. Ricardo Hausmann, Laura D. Tyson, and Saadia Zahidi, *The Global Gender Gap Report 2009*, World Economic Forum, https://members.weforum.org/pdf/gendergap/report2009.pdf (accessed July 28, 2011).
5. Amelia Forczak, "Is Your Organization Subconsciously Perpetuating the Gender Wage Gap?," HR Solutions eNews, December 2010, http://www.hrsolutionsinc.com/
6. Joseph Grenny, "The Downside of Virtual Teams." *Talent Management*, February 6, 2010, http://talentmgt.com/articles/view/the_downside_of_virtual_teams (accessed July 28, 2011).
7. Amelia Forczak, "Addressing Conflict without Confrontation," *HR Solutions eNews*, July 2010, http://www.hrsolutionsinc.com/enews_0710/Addressing_Conflict_0710.html.
8. Bureau of Labor Statistics, "Union Members—2010," U.S. Department of Labor, Bureau of Labor Statistics, January 21, 2011, http://www.bls.gov/news.release/union2.nr0.htm (accessed July 29, 2011).
9. Federation of European Employers, "Trade Unions across Europe," Federation of European Employers' website, http://www.fedee.com/tradeunions.html. (accessed July 29, 2011).
10. Kevin Sheridan and Kristina Anderson, "The Difference in Engagement and Satisfaction between Unionized and Non-

Unionized Employees," *HR Solutions eNews*, March 2011, http://www.hrsolutionsinc.com/enews_0311/Unionized_0311.html.

Chapter 6

1. U.S. Equal Employment Opportunity Commission, "Religion-Based Charges FY 1997–FY 2010," http://www.eeoc.gov/eeoc/statistics/enforcement/religion.cfm (accessed August 9, 2011).
2. DiversityInc, "About The DiversityInc Top 50 Companies for Diversity," February 22, 2011, http://www.diversityinc.com/article/8317/About-The-DiversityInc-Top-50-Companies-for-Diversity (accessed August 8, 2011).
3. Interview with Terri Dorsey, August 8, 2011.
4. HR Solutions' National Normative Database, https://actionpro.hrsolutionsinc.com (normative items; accessed May 25, 2011).
5. Job Accommodation Network, "Workplace Accommodations: Low Cost, High Impact," U.S. Department of Labor's Office of Disability Employment Policy, September 1, 2010, http://askjan.org/media/LowCostHighImpact.doc. (accessed August 9, 2011).
6. Interview with Teresa Clark, August 8, 2011.
7. Interview with Cynthia Trudell, June 2, 2011.
8. Bureau of Labor Statistics, "Employment and Earnings," U.S. Department of Labor, Bureau of Labor Statistics, January 2011, http://www.bls.gov/cps/cpsa2010.pdf (accessed August 9, 2011).
9. Brad Karsh's "What's My Job?" speech, presented on January 20, 2011 at the Employee Engagement Emporium event hosted by HR Solutions.
10. Interview with Brad Karsh, April 21, 2011.
11. Associated Press, "College Students Think They're So Special," msnbc.com, February 27, 2007, http://www.msnbc.msn.com/id/17349066/ns/health-mental_health/t/college-students-think-theyre-so-special (accessed August 9, 2011).

Chapter 7

1. HR Solutions' National Normative Database, https://actionpro.hrsolutionsinc.com (normative items; accessed May 25, 2011).

2. Amelia Forczak, "Fun Linked to Engagement," *HR Solutions eNews*, June 2010, http://www.hrsolutionsinc.com/enews_0610/Fun_Linked_to_Engagement_0610.html.
3. Amelia Forczak, "Client Spotlight—Radio Flyer," *HR Solutions eNews*, October 2010, http://www.hrsolutionsinc.com/enews_1010/RadioFlyer_1010.html.
4. Interview with Dan Jessup, July 5, 2011.
5. Amelia Forczak, "Do Employees Have to Dress Professionally to Act Professionally?" *HR Solutions eNews*, November 2010, http://www.hrsolutionsinc.com/enews_1110/DressCode_1110.html.
6. HR Solutions' National Normative Database, https://actionpro.hrsolutionsinc.com (normative items; accessed May 25, 2011).
7. Michael C. Fina, "Taking Initiative—How to Engage Your Workforce in 2011," *HR Solutions eNews*, April 2011, http://www.hrsolutionsinc.com/enews_0411/Taking_Initiative_0411.html.
8. Charles "Chic" Thompson, *What a* Great *Idea!* (New York: Harper Perennial, 1992), 26.
9. Kristina Anderson, "When It Comes to Building Engagement, Take Stress Out of the Workplace," *HR Solutions eNews*, February 2011, http://www.hrsolutionsinc.com/enews_0211/Job_Stress_0211.html.
10. Joan C. Williams and Heather Boushey, "The Three Faces of Work-Family Conflict," Center for American Progress, January 25, 2010, http://www.americanprogress.org/issues/2010/01/three_faces_report.html (accessed June 30, 2011).
11. Robert Half International and CareerBuilder.com, "Executive Summary: A Tale of Two Job Markets," *The EDGE Report*, September 2008, http://www.rhi.com/External_Sites/downloads/RHI/PressReleases/EDGE_Report_08-2008.pdf (accessed August 10, 2011).
12. Towers Watson, "2010 Global Workforce Study," 2010.
13. Ibid.
14. Interview with Suzanne Fallender, June 3, 2011.
15. Interview with Kathrin Winkler, May 23, 2011.

Chapter 8

1. Mike Byam, "Building a WOW! Recognition Culture," Terryberry, http://www.yvhra.org/Portals/0/January%20

Program%20-%20Building%20a%20WOW%20Recognition%20 Culture.pdf. (accessed September 16, 2011).

2. Reprinted with permission from the American Society for Healthcare Human Resources Administration (ASHHRA). Amelia Forczak, "Recognition: The Key Driver of Employee Engagement," *ASHHRA e-News Brief*, April 12, 2011, http://www.naylornetwork.com/ahh-nwl/articles/index-v2.asp?aid=141503&issueID=22503.
3. Interview with Mike Gamson, June 9, 2011.
4. Quote of Althea C. Lyons, sent via e-mail by NHC's PR manager, May 3, 2011.
5. Michael P. Savitt, "Client Focus: Northeast Hospital Corporation (NHC)," *HR Solutions eNews*, March 2011, http://www.hrsolutionsinc.com/enews_0311/Client_Focus_0311.html.
6. HR Solutions' National Normative Database, https://actionpro.hrsolutionsinc.com (normative items; accessed May 25, 2011).
7. Robert Reiss "Creating TouchPoints at Campbell Soup Company," Forbes.com, July 14, 2011, http://www.forbes.com/sites/robertreiss/2011/07/14/creating-touchpoints-at-campbell-soup-company/.
8. Interview with Jackie Scanlan, June 12, 2011.
9. The Humane Society of the United States, "U.S. Pet Ownership Statistics," The Humane Society of the United States, December 30, 2009, http://www.humanesociety.org/issues/pet_overpopulation/facts/pet_ownership_statistics.html. (accessed August 11, 2011).

INDEX

Note: Boldface page numbers indicate illustrations.

ABOUT THE AUTHOR

Kevin Sheridan is Chief Engagement Officer (CEO) and Chief Consultant of HR Solutions, Inc., a human capital management consulting firm specializing in employee engagement survey and exit survey design, implementation, analysis, and results. Sheridan has extensive experience in the field, having cofounded three successful survey-related organizations. He lives with his wife and two daughters in Chicago's North Shore.